THE BACK DOOR PEOPLE

BARBARA BRASETH JOHNSON

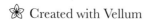

For my family

CONTENTS

Introduction   vii

Prologue   1

PART I
THE BACK DOOR HALF HOUSE

1. The Back Door Half House   5
2. Simple Pleasures   15
3. Sunday Afternoons at our Grandparents   21
4. Making Ends Meet   31
5. Sunday School   37
6. The Valentine's Day Party   43
7. Kindergarten   49

PART II
THE FRONT DOOR HALF HOUSE

8. The Front Door Half House   59
9. Unfamiliar Territory   67

PART III
THE HOUSE UP NORTH

10. The House Up North   75
11. The Mystery Box from Aunt Bertha   83
12. The Shopping Trip   87
13. Best Friends Ever   91

PART IV
THE SLUKEY HOUSE

14. The Slukey House   101

15. The Blue and White Bicycle   113
16. Piano Lessons and Porcupine Meatballs   123
17. A Surprise   129
18. A Tale of Two Blizzards   135

PART V
THE HOUSE WE BOUGHT
19. The House We Bought   145
20. My First Real Job   153
21. My First Driver's License   159
22. The Scholarship   163
23. Paying it Forward   175

A Brief Family History   181
Acknowledgments   193

INTRODUCTION

My childhood memories are all shelved away in my mind in volumes called houses—houses with names—the houses we lived in when I was growing up in the Great Depression Era. Like books on a library shelf, I have given each one an identifying title: The Back Door Half House, The Front Door Half House, The House Up North, The Slukey House, and The House We Bought.

Each house we lived in had a location which determined who our neighbors and playmates were (no arranged play-dates by protective mothers), how far we walked to school and Sunday school (for indeed, we did walk). It determined how far we carried the groceries when we did errands for our mother, and whether or not we had to face heel-nipping dogs or intimidating bullies.

By the time I was twelve years old, we had lived in five houses (if you count shifting from one half of a house to the other half), each one holding a volume of memories and pages of experiences that helped shape who I was becoming. Each house was more than a place of shelter. It was a place where we felt secure and cared for, a place where we belonged, a setting for our memories and emotions and for traditions lived out. And in those early years, a place from which Father went forth to work and Mother stayed home to nurture.

These are my memories of my childhood, written now as I am 85 years old. In my mind they are accurate, but sometimes my sisters, one older and one younger, didn't remember the same situation as I did. With their input, sometimes I adjusted facts and figures (especially how much something cost), but mostly I was just sure I was right. Memories can be like that. When we rehearse vague recollections in our minds, we can turn fiction into facts.

My story is not a dramatic story. It is merely recalling how life was lived in Northern Minnesota by a family struggling to make ends meet in the Depression Era, living before the age of technology, doing with less, finding our way day by day.

When I was about ten years old, my sister Betty accused me in a tone of disgust, "Oh you are such a Pollyanna!" Pollyanna was the "glad girl" who was always optimistic regardless of circumstance. I plead guilty. Even though I was shy and introverted, I had a happy nature. No doubt that happy nature slanted how I remembered places and events. And so I gladly share my memories of growing up in the Depression Era.

Barbara Braseth Johnson

PROLOGUE

TIMES WERE HARD IN NORWAY IN THE MID-1800S. WORD WAS coming from America that land was free to settlers through the Homestead Act, signed in 1862 by Abraham Lincoln. For the price of a small filing fee, immigrants could be given 160 acres of homestead land. After living there for five years, the homestead would be theirs.

Two of those homesteads were on opposite sides of the south branch of the Wild Rice River in Hagen Township, Ulen, Minnesota. My father, Lewis Braseth, was born in 1903 in the homestead on one side of that river, and my mother, Eleanor Wang, was born in 1907 in the homestead on the other side.

Lewis and Eleanor, those two farm kids, fell in love and married, and lived with Lewis' parents for the first year. After their first daughter, Betty, was born, they moved briefly to Moorhead, and then settled in Twin Valley, Minnesota, where I was born. An auto mechanic job *attracted my dad to the neighboring town of Mahnomen, so we moved when I was three and Betty was five. It was here that my childhood memories were formed.*

I

THE BACK DOOR
HALF HOUSE

1

THE BACK DOOR HALF HOUSE

A HOUSE GETS IT NAME IN RETROSPECT. WHEREVER WE LIVED, we called it "home," but when we looked back and wanted to differentiate between houses, we gave them names. Our first house in Mahnomen came to be named The Back Door Half House. That's because it actually was half a house—a duplex that was not originally built to be a two-family home. The front door, a large living room/kitchen, and the upstairs belonged to the other renters. We had the downstairs, and our entrance was the back door of the house. It was there that in my mind we first became The Back Door People.

We shared the house with a kind older couple, Carl Johnson, a blacksmith, and his wife Minnie, a loving, plump lady. Shortly after we were settled in, they broke the news to my parents that they had accomplished their dream. They had made a down payment on a small house in the north end of

Mahnomen and would soon be moving. I remember our family visiting them after their move, sensing their pride in their new home, and wondering who would replace them.

The new renters represented a class of society that was new to our sheltered lives. They were the Kimballs, a family of four, a couple with a boy and a girl who were a little older than we were. Like our father, Gordon Kimball, an autobody expert, worked at Roy's Garage and Machine Shop. But unlike our father, he cleaned up and dressed up when he was through with work for the day. Mr. Kimball was tall and slender and had a mustache. His trim wife dressed fancy by our standards, used a lot of makeup and smoked cigarettes, something that was totally foreign to us. They probably were accustomed to more than half a house, or at least they looked like they came from a life different from ours.

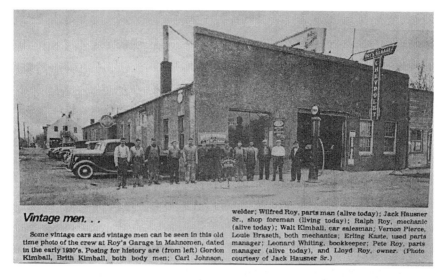

Vintage men. . .

Some vintage cars and vintage men can be seen in this old time photo of the crew at Roy's Garage in Mahnomen, dated in the early 1930's. Posing for history are (from left) Gordon Kimball, Brith Kimball, both body men; Carl Johnson, welder; Wilfred Roy, parts man (alive today); Jack Hausner Sr., shop foreman (living today); Ralph Roy, mechanic (alive today); Walt Kimball, car salesman; Vernon Pierce, Louie Braseth, both mechanics; Erling Kaste, used parts manager; Leonard Whiting, bookkeeper; Pete Roy, parts manager (alive today), and Lloyd Roy, owner. (Photo courtesy of Jack Hausner Sr.)

Roy's Garage and Machine Shop and all its employees. My dad is 5th from the right. Clipping from Mahnomen Pioneer Newspaper.

The temporary plywood divider erected in the archway separated their living room from ours, with the furnace grate spanning the area, giving off heat for both families. If we stood on the outer rim of our half of the square furnace grate, we could feel the heat coming up without burning our feet. On cold winter days, we scampered out of bed, grabbed our clothes and dressed while balancing on the edge of the furnace grate, sometimes standing there until the heat forced us off.

My dad took the responsibility of tending the furnace, which heated both halves of the house. Coal was delivered periodically through a basement window, tumbling down a coal chute into a sectioned-off place called a coal bin, ready to be hand shoveled into the furnace. I remember the term "bank the coals," which meant to make sure the coals were alive all night. By morning the house had cooled off somewhat, and my dad would go to the basement and "stoke the furnace"—use a poker to stir up the coals, adding more if necessary.

The furnace, a big round-bellied, metal monster that was fed coal, sat in the dark basement, with a single light bulb dangling by a braided cord from the ceiling, providing some much-needed light. Sometimes I followed my dad part-way down to the basement through the door from the kitchen, going down two steps to the landing, turning and going down three more steps, and then sitting on the open stairway and watching as he tended the furnace. From my position sitting on the steps, I could also see the light reflecting off my mother's canning jars, filled with yellow peaches or green beans, all lined up on shelves on the other side of the room in that mysterious, dirt-floored place that some people called the cellar. As he opened the door of the furnace with his coal-dust stained, yellow flannel work gloves, I could see the coals burning red and orange. He used the poker to stir them, causing the flames to lick out of the open door. In a rhythmic movement, he shoveled coal from the coal bin into the furnace, shut the door, and as he took off his gloves and left them behind on the workbench, he turned to come back upstairs, saying to me: "Come along."

MY PARENTS HAD their own bedroom and even had a clothes closet. It was the best-furnished room in the house after my mother bought her four-piece bedroom set with money saved nickel-by-nickel out of the grocery allowance. Besides the double bed, there was a tall, waterfall-front, varnished four-drawer dresser and a vanity and a bench to sit on. The vanity had a large round mirror and a flat surface supported on each end by a set of drawers, with a drawer in the middle. Mother's beautiful pearl-backed brush, hand mirror, and comb set looked grand on that vanity if you didn't turn it over and see the crack in the glass from when I dropped it. (Did she scold me? Not really, but I could tell that she was disappointed because she didn't have many pretty things.) An upholstered bench fit under the vanity when it was not in use.

The furniture in our living room featured a daybed with

sagging springs that served as a couch during the day but was opened out for bedtime, and this is where Betty and I slept. I remember quarreling over the space and one telling the other: "DON'T go over the center line!" Or tattling to Mother: "Mom, she is on my side." And Mother would say, "Now, girls, learn to get along."

THE KITCHEN FLOOR was covered with linoleum that had moved with us from Twin Valley. On moving day, it had been packed on top of an open, fully-loaded truck, and we followed behind in our car. I remember my fear as a three-year old when I watched it fall off the truck in front of us, and my relief when my dad rescued it after it rolled into the ditch. I was alarmed at seeing it fall, but I felt like my Dad could do anything. He took care of the matter, and we got it safely re-loaded. Now it was on our kitchen floor.

The wood-burning stove, referred to as "the range" was the queen of the kitchen, standing like a high-bosomed, wide-bellied matron whose skirt reached down to her claw-like feet. She served us well in all the houses in which we lived until we finally remodeled the house we owned after I graduated from college. Her smooth, black metal cooking surface with four burners was heated by the fire below, and when more heat was needed, wood could be added by inserting a handle into the cover to lift it off. A wide oven below produced much aromatic homemade bread, double warming ovens above were used for storage, and a water reservoir on the end kept hot water available.

Sweetheart wood cookstove with water reservoir. From the Heartland Classic Collection.

My first memory of my baby sister, Patty, revolves around that stove. She was about two years old and had been playing outdoors and wanted Mother's food strainer to sift some sand in the sandbox. Unable to find someone to help her at the moment, she pushed a chair up to our big cooking range, and climbed up, standing on the flat surface of the cookstove in her scuffed high-topped leather shoes to get the strainer out of the warming oven above the stove. Success!

The pain came when she climbed down and needed to sit down on the stove to get back to the chair. The stove was still hot from dinner preparations, and since her colorful, short print dress and panties did not provide much protection from the heat, she burned her tender bottom. It took a moment or two for her to realize what she was feeling, but then she screamed as she sat helpless on the hot stove. If this were today, she would have been rushed off to the emergency room, but back then, her injury was likely not considered severe enough to see a doctor—not much was that serious in those days. She doesn't even have scars from it. Just a bad memory that even she can recall, and a cautionary tale to tell her grandchildren.

Our icebox was actually a free-standing insulated cupboard designed to keep our milk and other foods cold with the help of a block of ice placed on the shelf at the top. I understand there was an ice delivery man who delivered ice daily, but I don't actually remember much about it. We depended on this icebox until we moved to the House Up North several years later. A sink mounted on the wall provided us with running water, but the complete bathroom was upstairs and belonged to the Front Door renters.

IN THE MIDDLE of the kitchen stood a white enamel-top table which seated the five of us for meals three times a day. My dad always walked home from work for the noon meal, and once we were in school we also walked home to eat at noon. This was dinner for us, the biggest meal of the day. It often consisted of potatoes, either boiled or fried, and some kind of meat from the store, freshly caught fish, or wild game provided by a hunting trip.

I later realized that my mother willingly helped clean the pheasants or ducks or fish because they put food on the table without straining the food budget. We had vegetables from the garden in season or from what Mother put up in canning jars. Other favorites included tasty goulash made from hamburger and macaroni and canned tomatoes. We would often have oatmeal or eggs or pancakes for breakfast or supper.

As we sat around the table, my dad leaned over his plate and concentrated on eating so he could get back to work. My mother loved hot coffee and black pepper, but my father did not share these loves. If he was served peppery food, he complained. Other than that, his palate was easy to please as long as it was simple food he recognized and the temperature of his food was not too hot.

THE LONG DIRT driveway with the compacted tire tracks and the garage with the sagging doors were also ours, which was good because we had a car. I think it was a squarish-looking Chevrolet, but there is no one still alive who remembers. Of course, a mechanic would have a car, even a financially-strapped mechanic who was struggling to provide for his young family. Behind the garage was the outhouse—a two-holer — equipped with an older version of the Sears Roebuck catalog for toilet paper.

It was here in the back yard where we gravitated to play

—after all, we were The Back Door People. A large, gnarled oak tree with branches low enough for us to climb stood in the back corner of the property, sometimes serving as a ship that carried us to faraway places, sometimes serving as Noah's ark.

This was the house where, in my imagination, Little Women lived. The characters in another favorite book, The Five Little Peppers, also grew up here, and I believed that the ingredients for the raisin cake they made when they were very poor came out of our very own cupboard. And while I am at it, I may as well tell you that the big bad wolf from Little Red Riding Hood slept in my parents' $39 bedroom set. Who would have guessed the houses could contain such memories that never actually happened?

Betty, Patty, me, and a neighbor boy, Snookie Agnew, in the front yard of the Back Door Half House.

❦   2   ❦

SIMPLE PLEASURES

SOMETIMES THE SIMPLE PLEASURES ARE WHAT WE REMEMBER with the greatest fondness. One of my great delights was to roller skate in our house. Our roller skates were not shoe skates. They were made of tarnished silver-colored metal, shaped like the sole of a shoe, with metal extensions on each side of the ball of the foot that would be clamped unto our leather shoes. A key was required to tighten the skates to hold them securely, and a leather strap buckled around the ankle.

The sidewalk in front of our house was somewhat cracked and broken up, with the surface a bit rough, so it was hard to get much momentum while skating there, so sometimes Mother let us roller skate on the kitchen floor—on that rescued linoleum. How very smooth and pleasurable it was to skate alongside the white, enamel-topped kitchen table, grabbing the edge of the sink which was mounted to the wall to help us turn, and then gain speed as we pushed off the other side of the table, sailing through the doorway into the living room, and turning around when we reached the daybed to repeat the route again. Mother cleaned the kitchen floor after every meal, so we sensed she took pride in her kitchen space. Skating was noisy, of course, and we innately knew that we should not overdo it. If Mother got perturbed because it was past her tolerance level, we might never be able to do it again. So we wisely quit before she said, "No more of that!" As an adult, I reminded her of the great pleasure of skating in the kitchen, and she said, "Well, you kids didn't have much, so at least you could have that pleasure."

Another simple pleasure was milk delivery. The milkman regularly delivered quart-size glass bottles of milk to an insulated box sitting outside our back door. We put the empty bottles out and he left the same number of filled bottles. Whole milk always separated with the cream rising to the top, and Mother skimmed that off for whipping cream which she used for special treats. I especially remember the frozen milk in the winter. Milk was delivered early in the morning, and on the coldest of winter days it sat there long enough to freeze. As it expanded, it pushed out of the bottle, forcing the cap off, creating a white mountain of crystals sitting on top. I begged to taste those frozen crystals—it was a little like ice cream, which, of course, was one of the really great pleasures of childhood, a treat provided by Mother Nature and the milkman.

We made our own fun. Not only was the new Sears Roebuck catalog a valuable reference book for the entire family—you could find a picture and description of most anything in the catalog—it was a source for paper dolls. We cut out the head and shoulders of a model in the catalog and then found other pictures to cut out outfits for her (and him). We also furnished houses for the paper dolls from the furniture section of the catalog. Our imaginations ran wild with such fine things. The catalog was sometimes referred to as a "wish book," but I don't remember that we yearned for any of those things. It was a separate life and didn't have anything to do with me except something to play with.

Sometimes a simple pleasure was just a moment of connection. I remember the smell of my dad's greasy blue and white striped overalls when he came home for dinner every noon. When he was in a playful mood, sometimes I stood on the toes of his heavy work shoes, facing him, and he held my hands in his and helped me walk up his legs, almost up to the silver metal embossed buttons on his bib overalls, and then flip over. A few repeats of this activity, and then it was time for him to walk the four blocks back to work.

Saturday afternoon baths were not necessarily fun, but what followed bath time was one of our highlights of the week. Although there was a bathroom in the house, it was upstairs and belonged to the family who rented the other half of the house. We would be the front-door people later in that very house, but for now, my mother heated water on the range in a copper boiler, and placed a square, galvanized washtub on the kitchen floor, filling it with hot water for our baths. We all used the same water, taking turns, ending with a shampoo.

Over the years it became a tradition after our baths—wearing clean clothes and bows in our hair—to go to the library to pick out books for the week. The library at that time was several blocks away in the upstairs of a musty, dusty building at the end of Main Street. The building didn't have any appeal in itself, but it held great treasures for us. When we left the library with our arms filled with books, we often stopped at the ice cream store and spent a nickel on a treat. We had two choices: a triple ice cream cone, or a small chocolate sundae in a paper cup that was called a "little Dick."

We sometimes went for family rides around town in the evening, driving slowly, looking this way and that, checking out what was going on in the neighborhoods of our small town. Every once in a while, our rides ended with stopping at the store and buying a pint of Neapolitan ice cream to be shared around the kitchen table when we got home. My mother would open out the waxy cardboard container and lay it flat, revealing a slightly melting block of ice cream. Using a long knife, she would slice through the chocolate, strawberry, and vanilla stripes, dividing it into four (or five) pieces, one for each family member, dishing it into cereal bowls, making sure each one got some of each flavor. We did not have a refrigerator, and the icebox could not keep anything frozen. We could have purchased ice cream cones but sharing a pint of ice cream was more economical—and that was always taken into consideration.

Street scene, Mahnomen Minnesota, 1940's. Courtesy LakesnWoods.com
Postcard and Postcard Image Collection

My Dad worked long hours from Monday to Saturday, but on Saturday nights he took a break. He would drive the car three blocks to the uptown main street and find a good parking place, preferably in front of the grocery store, and then walk home. After supper we would walk uptown and sit in the car and watch people go by. Sometimes my sister and I would see friends and jump out of the car and walk arm in arm, locking elbows, up and down the streets with them. This would be the time to buy heavy items like 25-pound sacks of flour or 10 pounds of sugar, so we could take it home in the car. My mother would settle up her bill at the L.B. Hartz Grocery Store, where she had charged groceries all week. The store owner would add up her bill, and if she could pay in full, he would throw in a candy bar or two.

Roller skating in the house...tasting frozen milk crystals and ice cream...paper dolls from the Sears Roebuck Wish-book…getting books from the library…going for a ride in the family car. As I look back, I am reminded that life was full of pleasures. We just had to look for them.

3

SUNDAY AFTERNOONS AT OUR GRANDPARENTS

ON SUNDAY AFTERNOONS WE WOULD OFTEN DRIVE THIRTY-FIVE miles into the countryside near Ulen, Minnesota, to visit both sets of grandparents, who still lived across the river from each other, first a visit to one and then to the other.

At my dad's home place, the farm buildings sat high above the river. I knew it as Grandma and Grandpa Braseth's House, but it first belonged to my great grandmother, Gunhild Haug, the widow who had built the house with the help of neighbors on this Homestead Land. It was a two-story building with white siding that housed a very large kitchen, two parlors (one that was used regularly and one with a closed door), and a bedroom on the first floor. I remember a settee with a horsehide rug over the back, which my dad likely preserved from the hide of one of their own horses. I sat on the edge of that settee, not having any desire to cozy up to that horsehide rug. Other furnishings I remember were my grandpa's chair, a table with a lot of green houseplants and a china cabinet with curved glass doors. If we stayed late enough in the afternoon, when the sun was setting, and the lighting was too dim for reading, it would be time to light the kerosene lamps. It was kind of a cozy feeling that it was soon the end of the day.

The Braseth homestead, taken before Lewis was born

There was a phone mounted on the wall in the kitchen. When the phone rang, it was not necessarily for any of us. Each family had to know their own signal. The ring for the

Braseth home was two short rings and one long one. It was possible to listen in on everyone's phone conversations to find out what the neighbors were doing. It was so fascinating to me because we didn't even have a telephone in our home yet.

The parlor with the closed door housed a pump organ from which music could be coaxed if one could coordinate pumping with the feet while playing the keyboard. Betty was intrigued with the pump organ, and Grandma Braseth said she could have it, but the transaction was never finalized. It would require some heavy-duty transportation to get that to Mahnomen. A little girl could never manage to get that done without a lot of help, so it remained on the farm. It was probably just as well for all the times we moved, and the small quarters we lived in, but Betty never forgot that pump organ.

Another building that I remember was a cook shanty, a one-room building about twenty feet from the main house which was used in the summertime as a substitute kitchen so the main house would remain cool. I have fond memories of sitting around the table with Grandma, Uncle Clifford, and my family in that cook shanty at afternoon lunchtime with

Our Grandma and Grandpa Braseth
—Bendick and Lise Braseth

the windows open and the curtains gently moving in the summer breeze. Minnesota summers were pleasant.

An icehouse stored huge chunks of ice which had been cut from the frozen river the previous winter. Packed in sawdust and still frozen solid in midsummer, they were available to chill whatever was in Grandma's icebox. Much later, when my mother was reminiscing, she told how Grandma Braseth had raised turkeys, cleaned them and packed them in ice from this icehouse, and shipped them to business places in Chicago. She was quite an entrepreneur—I have no idea how she made those business connections. They did have a phone, and she did have able-bodied sons who could haul barrels to the train station. I wish I had asked more questions when there was someone who could answer.

Behind the cook shanty grew a huge patch of rhubarb, memorable for the quantity and the size of the plants. A little further on below a steep embankment, the Wild Rice River flowed steadily, pushing up against and rippling around a variety of stones randomly placed by Mother Nature in the river. We played on these stones, jumping from one stone to the next, all the way to the other side of the river, risking falls because some were slippery.

Then hastily we returned again for fear there were animals in the woods on the other side. We knew our dad had killed a bobcat in those woods because it stood in Grandma's attic, preserved with his taxidermy skills when he was in his early twenties. Its yellow eyes stared above an open mouth full of sharp teeth, never moving its yellowish-brown furry body from its tense position. We knew it couldn't hurt us but were still reluctant to get very close to it.

A little farther downstream the river banks had eroded, creating a habitat that attracted cliff swallows which swooped in and out of their nests. We had never seen anything like it. Because it felt strange to us, we didn't play there very long. Soon our parents were calling us because it was time to visit our other grandparents.

MY MOTHER'S CHILDHOOD HOME, the Wang farm, was across the bridge on the other side of the river. I knew it as Grandma and Grandpa Wang's House, but it was actually not the house built on that Homestead Land. The original house burned down after my mother was married, so my grandparents purchased this house from Grandpa's widowed mother, Ellen Wang, and moved the house five miles from Ulen with tractors. It was a big, two-story, white wooden frame house with a decorative oval window on the right side of the front.

We always entered the back door into Grandma's kitchen, which was furnished much like ours with the big cooking range, the icebox, the cupboard in the corner. There was a wood box near the stove and drinking water with a dipper in a big crock nearby. A washstand with a hand pump filled another corner of the room.

The dining room had an oval table which could be made bigger with extensions for holiday meals. Patty and I remember being squeezed between adults at those family meals, which seemed to be occasions for eating, and not much conversation. But that was okay, because the food was delicious and plentiful. And if aunts and uncles and cousins came to Grandma's for a holiday, a second setting at the table was necessary.

Ellen Wang's house being moved by tractors to the Wang homestead

THERE WERE two parlors in this house also, one for everyday use and one behind glass doors. This special parlor became a bedroom for "the old gramma" when she could no longer navigate the stairs. After reading the history of this family, I realize that "the old gramma" was the original owner of this house, Grandpa Bernard Wang's mother. Now she was being cared for by them, and they were living in her house, the house that was moved to this farm. She had memory problems, perhaps Alzheimer's, and periodically would pack her chamber pot with clothes and run away into the woods. As soon as her absence was discovered, everyone would go searching for her to bring her back to safety. When she died, I remember a feeling of awe as I saw her dead body in a coffin in that front parlor awaiting the time for the funeral.

We always snooped in the bedrooms upstairs. Three of them were neatly but sparsely furnished. The doors of the other two rooms were locked, so we were left to our imaginations as to what was in them. As children, we tried staying overnight in this house more than once, but we always got homesick. We loved being here when we knew our parents were safely downstairs and that we would be going home with them.

Something unique about the Wang farm was a huge woodpile halfway between the house and the red barn. It was stacked round and round like a cylindrical building with wood that was chopped and ready for the stove. Apparently whenever he didn't have more pressing farm chores, Grandpa Wang chopped wood. The barn and a machine shop bordered the yard. A herd of cows were kept in a fenced-in pasture by day and brought into the barn for milking in the evening. I still remember the smell of milk whenever we went into the building near the kitchen that housed the cream separator.

Large oak and maple trees shaded the paths down into the wooded areas towards the river where we would play house with items we found in the dirt. It looked as if someone had played there before us. We wondered if the broken, discarded dishes had previously been played with by our Aunt Frances when she was a little girl. At the river we played on the stepping stones, mentally measuring if we could safely jump to the next stone. Sometimes we crossed the river and pretended we were explorers, but we dared not venture too far for fear we would not know the way back.

At whichever grandparents' house we were at midafternoon, there would be a lunch of homemade buns with meat or cheese, a huge glass bowl of home-canned peaches, served into sauce dishes with a wide serving ladle, and usually a plate of sugar cookies. There was a feeling of abundance.

Our Grandpa and Grandma Wang—
Bernard and Clara Wang

Both sets of grandparents were alike in that they patted us on the head as a token of recognition that we existed, sometimes declared that we were "nice girls," and then went on with the adult conversation. We didn't mind. We enjoyed the freedom to play and explore.

Sometimes we would fall asleep in the car on the way home, and our parents would carry us in and put us to bed while we were still sleeping. Visiting grandparents on a Sunday afternoon was an enjoyable part of life as it began in the Back Door Half House, our first home in Mahnomen.

❧ 4 ❧

MAKING ENDS MEET

Radio similar to the one our family often gathered around.

OUR RADIO[1] WAS A SPECIAL connection to the outside world. I quite clearly remember my parents listening with the utmost respect to President Roosevelt's Fireside chats. According to an internet report, he delivered thirty chats between March 1933 and June 1944 and reached an astonishing number of American households, 90 percent of which owned a radio at the time. President Roosevelt used simple vocabulary and relied on folksy stories to explain the complex issues facing the country. I could sense the deep respect my parents had for President Roosevelt and that they felt reassured because he was at the helm of the nation. What a wonderful feeling it was to have the people united behind their leader and no one publicly criticizing the government in the media.

When President Roosevelt took office in 1933, the country was wallowing in the Great Depression, and people couldn't find work. There was a run on the bank, and the president declared a "bank holiday," which meant that he shut the bank system down for a week.

I was too young to understand the conditions of the country at the time, but as I looked back and also as I heard my parents talk about it, I knew that his reassuring voice told them that everything was going to be all right. The banks were going to be reliable and would re-open, their money was safe, that there would be jobs created and food available for those who needed help.

My parents probably did not have money in the bank—more likely in my Dad's billfold or in a sock or under the mattress. My Dad always had a job, and he worked long hard hours for $25 a week. We just knew by their attitudes that they would never apply for relief—that was for destitute people.

Mother was an accomplished seamstress and made most of our clothes with the Singer treadle sewing machine that would follow us from house to house. One of her prized possessions, the machine head was folded down into a wooden cabinet which rested on fancy wrought-iron legs. The cabinet had an attached wooden leaf hinged and folded over it. When Mother got ready to sew, she removed the sewing basket and button box sitting on top, lifted the wooden leaf, positioning it out to the left where it became workspace, and then lifted the head of the machine, which swung into place. The cabinet was built with two drawers on each side with leg room in the middle to operate the treadle with one's foot, which powered the machine. The drawers were filled with colorful spools of thread, needles, pieces of elastic, buttons and miscellaneous sewing supplies.

A 1920s Singer Treadle sewing machine just like ours.
Courtesy of Cornell University Library

Mother sewed our dresses out of flour sacks, often trading with another seamstress so she could get more than one sack of a particular pattern—enough to make a child's dress. Very cleverly, she also recycled the fabric from a man's suit and created a woman's suit for my third-grade teacher, Miss Guptil. She did something similar for Mrs. Whiting, making a suit for Mary Kathryn from her dad's old suit. Her pay for that was the fabric from another discarded man's suit, which she could use for her own sewing projects.

Colorfully Printed Flour Sacks.
Creative Commons: Courtesy of Life
Magazine.

Looking back and having done some sewing myself, I realize how much work that really was: ripping, pressing sections of fabric and cutting it out, matching the plaids. But the material was high-quality wool, so it looked great in her finished product. She made her own patterns by looking and measuring from garments that fit. A fabric artist and a genius at being thrifty, she was always looking for ways to be creative and save money.

My mother managed each house we lived in, shopping for groceries, cooking, cleaning, washing clothes in the wringer washing machine, taking care of our clothing needs, and sewing our dresses from those colorful print flour sacks. She did it all on the allowance my Dad gave her of $25 a month.

She secretly stashed away nickels and dimes and quarters out of that allowance and eventually saved enough to buy their four-piece bedroom set, for which she paid the handsome price of $39. No wonder we sometimes had all-you-can-eat oatmeal or eggs for supper. Much later, her grown grandson would comment that she should have been put in charge of the national debt!

I remember visiting with my sisters when we were adults, and I commented,

"I didn't know we were poor when we were growing up."

Betty was astounded at my naïve statement.

"Incredulous! You didn't know we were poor?" she exclaimed.

I always felt like I had enough and was content. I didn't expect to have more. But I can understand Betty's perspective. For instance, she was the one who loved summer sausage, and the one piece she was given for supper was not enough for her. She used to put it on the center of her bread and ate towards it, and then kept moving it a little at a time so she could have some left for another piece of bread. She even asked for a whole summer sausage for Christmas one year. I guess one piece of summer sausage was enough for me.

Although times were uneasy and providing for two, and later three, children in that era had to be challenging, we as children didn't sense any fear or lack of confidence from our parents. If they wanted to talk about something they didn't want us to hear, they just spoke in Norwegian. I always felt protected and safe and cared for. And my older sister Betty?

She showed a little more spunk. She wanted to learn Norwegian!

---

1. Permission to use photograph. Picture taken by fir0002flagstaffotos [at] gmail.comCanon 20D + Tamron 28-75mm f/2.8.Own work, GFDL 1.2, https://commons.wikimedia.org/w/index.php?curid=210545

SUNDAY SCHOOL

IN MY PRE-SCHOOL YEARS, MY LIFE WAS MOSTLY SHELTERED from outside influences. We rarely had company or visited other homes, other than occasional visits to or from relatives. If it is true that we learn most by contrast, I realize we didn't have much to contrast with until we started to venture forth on our own. My first venture was to Sunday School.

Today, most parents don't want or expect their children to walk four blocks to Sunday School when they are four and six years old. My dad owned a car but used it rarely, mostly on weekly trips "back to the home place," which meant a trip to Grandma's. Sometimes we would take the car uptown on Saturday night as a place to sit and visit with people, or maybe go for a ride around town as a family. He would use it to go hunting or fishing. But giving the children a ride to

Sunday School on a rainy day was not a legitimate use for the car. We walked the four blocks, in good weather or not-so-good weather. And as we interacted with people, we learned that some adults are kind and some are not always kind.

When I was just four years old, I started attending Sunday School at the Lutheran Church with my sister Betty, and that was probably my earliest, strongest sense of "contrast." Betty was already established as a Sunday school student and enjoyed her role as big sister.

Mother urged us along, "Girls, it is time to get going if you are going to get to Sunday School on time. Do you have your offering? Betty, take Barbara's hand and help her find her class. You remember where the four-year-olds sit." Hand in hand, we skipped along on the sidewalk past the public school, past the Knights of Columbus Hall.

KC Hall, Mahnomen Minnesota, 1943 Courtesy
LakesnWoods.com Postcard and Postcard Image Collection

If it was another day besides Sunday, we might stop to climb the steps and slide down the wide cement railing, which wore holes in our panties, but this was Sunday, so we kept going.

We went past two more blocks of houses, and there stood the church on the opposite side of the street on the corner, large and white, with a steeple on top.

Betty said that Sunday school students went in the back door, so we crossed the street and went around to the back entrance, pulling the heavy door open, and thumped down the stairs into the basement. Looking through the glass windows into the big gathering room, we could see the students moving about and settling into their areas by grade. Betty took me over to the section for preschoolers where we sat in small wooden chairs with armrests built in, painted various colors —red, green, yellow or blue, and then she found her way to her own section.

First Lutheran Church, Mahnomen Minnesota, 1962. Courtesy LakesnWoods.com Postcard and Postcard Image Collection

Our Sunday School superintendent was Harry Goodrich,

an older man with stern lips and unusually bushy eyebrows. He read the scriptures and led the songs from his position up front, standing near the upright varnished piano. He expected everyone to be quiet and attentive, and if anyone came in late, he stopped what he was saying and just waited until the embarrassed child had walked across the creaky floor and was seated, all eyes glancing from Mr. Goodrich to the child and back again to see what Mr. Goodrich would do. He would simply look up from the Bible he was reading, glaring from under his bushy eyebrows until the child was seated. Oh, how I hated being late!

For the older children, classes were held in curtained-off sections of the assembly room. Because of crowded conditions, we pre-schoolers moved our little painted chairs into the closet where the choir gowns were stored. As we listened to the teacher tell the Bible stories, I remember that cramped space with the bright blue silky choir gowns with white collars hanging on three sides of us. If it hadn't been for the calm, kind voice of our teacher Ellen Lokensgaard reading stories to us, it might have been a frightening experience.

And so we were introduced to the Bible stories at an early age: the Garden of Eden, which I imagined was in the tangled brush laced with wild cucumber vines behind our house; Noah's ark, which I pictured in the big tree in our back yard; and the story that Jesus was coming back. I remember sitting in the swing at home, twisting and turning slowly, getting my shoes dusty in the dirt below the swing, mulling it over, and asking God to please send Jesus back while I was still alive because I wanted to get in on the excitement. We were told that God answers prayers, especially those of innocent believing children, so take notice! Considering my age, it could be any time now.

❧ 6 ❧

THE VALENTINE'S DAY PARTY

THE YEAR WAS 1935. OUR COUNTRY WAS IN THE DEPRESSION Era. Patty was just a baby, I was four, and my sister Betty was six. We had been living in our first rental home in Mahnomen, Minnesota, for about a year. The major influences in my four years of life had been my parents, my sister Betty, my Sunday School teacher and classmates, and an occasional neighborhood playmate. I was set to have another experience of the outside world—I was going to visit school with my sister! Excited and full of anticipation, I could never have imagined that it would be anything less than wonderful. Nor could I have guessed that I would have an experience, the impact of which would take me until just recently to understand fully.

Betty, now a first grader, was a sturdily built little girl, an extrovert, with brown hair and hazel eyes. In contrast, I was thin and pale, blue-eyed with blond hair which was blunt-cut in a bob, an introvert, shy, sensitive. Betty would often bring home papers and books from school to practice reading. I couldn't wait until I "got big" so I could go to school and learn to read.

Then in early February, Betty's teacher announced that the first graders were going to have a Valentine's party and they could bring a younger brother or sister. I was invited to go to school with my big sister!

We lived only a block from the school building. I had been intrigued with it for a long time—a huge, brick three-story building with lots of windows and three wide cement steps leading up to double doors that had push-down bars for handles. Inside those doors, there was a large staircase with worn, wooden steps, shabby from years of use—space for many students to enter or leave at the same time.

February 14 finally arrived! Mother sent us out the door together, hand in hand as much as thick mittens allowed, trudging up the snowy sidewalk in our overshoes. We wore brown stockings bulging in wrinkles over our long underwear. Our hand-me-down coats covered our home-made dresses, sewn out of colorful print flour sacks. Our mittens were secured by a knit cord through the sleeves of our coats so we wouldn't lose them, and knit caps snugly covered our ears.

Sometimes my rival, but today my protector, my sister Betty led me up the stairs of the school building, through the double doors, then across the hall into the first-grade class-room. We hung up our coats on hooks in the long coat hall, with our mittens hanging out the sleeves, then tucked our caps into one sleeve and placed our overshoes on the floor below our coats. Full of excitement and anticipation, yet a bit shy, I was wide-eyed as I entered the world of my big sister's classroom.

Mahnomen High School, Mahnomen Minnesota, 1915. Courtesy Minnesota Historical Society

The teacher's desk was over to one side in the front, and there were five rows of wooden desks with five desks in each row, each one fastened on long wooden slats with curlicue wrought iron braces, keeping them uniformly apart. Betty's desk was near the back in the second row. The desks had lift-up covers, so you could store books and papers and pencils and colors inside. There were blackboards on the front wall and on one side wall of the room, windows on one side, and bulletin boards on the back wall, filled with colorful pictures and artwork created by the students. It was quite wonderful to my four-year-old eyes.

Betty sat down in her desk and motioned me to sit beside her. There was much activity with first-graders getting settled. Then a bell rang, and everyone quieted down. The teacher was coming towards us. She looked so tall. She was not smiling. She was saying something to my sister:

"Betty, you were not supposed to bring your sister until the party this afternoon."

My heart sank and felt like a heavy weight in the pit of my stomach, and a sick feeling washed over me. *I wasn't supposed to be here.* I wanted to disappear, but there was no place to go. My tears were very close to the surface.

Betty's shoulders sagged, too, and she looked wide-eyed— what had just happened?

Either the first-grade teacher saw my reaction that day, or perhaps she was just being practical. How could she send a four-year-old child home alone—we had no phones to call mom. So she kindly said, "It is okay. Your sister can sit in the chairs at the back of the room."

And so I was allowed to stay all day in the place where someday I, too, would learn to read and to write cursive like the Palmer Method writing charts that lined the walls above the blackboards and would be called on by the teacher to read aloud or to answer questions.

I don't remember the Valentine's Day party at all. But I

clearly remember the sinking feeling of being where I was not supposed to be on that particular February day.

A child with a different temperament may well have said, "Oops, we goofed. That is funny. What do we do now?" But I was a tender-hearted pleaser and believed I had displeased someone who in my mind outranked even my mother. Because I tried so hard to be good, it was crushing to make a mistake.

So this venture into the world without the protection of my parents began with high expectation and innocence and ended in a huge letdown, one that I didn't quite understand.

Today, eighty-some years later, we are all living in a world that is much more "psychological." My daughter telephones daily just to chat. She asks me about my writing class and what memories I am recording now. When I tell her about the valentine's day visit to school, she identifies the feelings I experienced: "Mom, that is *shame*. You should listen to the TED talk by a woman named Brene' Brown on the internet. Just google it." And so I did. It was a revelation to me.

Brene' Brown's research shows that everyone experiences shame at various times of life—the feeling that one is trapped and cannot get away and does not measure up—is not good enough. She points out that shame grows when there is secrecy, silence, and judgment, and that the best antidote to shame is empathy. She concludes that we need to identify shame as the "swampland" it is and "put on our galoshes and wade through it and get to the other side."

In looking back, I recognize that the secrecy and silence

and judgment that feed shame and help it grow were in my own tender heart because I did not talk about my feelings and receive the healing powers of empathy.

The sneaky voice of Shame has spoken to me many times since that day when I was four years old, but I wasn't informed enough until recently to call him by name. Because I recognize him, he no longer has the same power over me. I now smile upon four-year-old Barbara and tell her it was a little misunderstanding, that I am sorry it happened to her, but that she is fine just the way she is.

In spite of that deflating experience on my first visit to school, I continued to look forward to the day when I could go to kindergarten and be a student day after day, year after year, for years to come. In fact, as I look back, I realize I spent most of my life in school, either as a student or a teacher. I loved school!

7

KINDERGARTEN

I STARTED KINDERGARTEN IN THE PUBLIC SCHOOL WHILE WE lived in the Back Door Half House—certainly a great location for a kindergartner to walk to school, just a block away. We did have some perceived threats from bullies that frightened Betty and me. When it was time to go to school in the mornings, we were afraid to walk the block to school if the bullies who lived across the street were in sight. Those boys knew they had power over us, and all they had to do was make a motion as if they were going to chase us, and we would run in terror. One solution was to walk behind the three houses in our block, cut through the neighbors' yards, and duck through holes in the hedges to get to school. We looked warily this way and that until we were safely within the building.

· · ·

ONE OF MY first memories of kindergarten involves a request from my teacher, asking us to bring an empty oatmeal box to school the next day if we could. As soon as I got home from school, I flung my coat on the chair, grabbed a bread and homemade plum jelly sandwich my mother had ready for me, and asked my mother,

"Do we have an empty oatmeal box I can bring to school tomorrow?" Actually, oatmeal was one of our main food groups, so it was not an unreasonable request. We ate it more often for supper than for breakfast, but we did consume a lot of oatmeal.

"Well, I suppose I could empty one and put the oatmeal in another container."

The next day I was so proud as I brought my oatmeal box to school and put it with the others on the table at the back of the room, thinking my teacher, Miss Reiter, would be so pleased.

During our nap time, Miss Reiter and the teacher's aide were in the back of the room, taking inventory of oatmeal boxes. I heard the teacher say:

"This one won't work. It doesn't have a cover. It would be impossible to make a drum out of a box without a cover. What were they thinking?"

I sneaked a peek to see which box they were talking about. It was the one I brought! No one had said what it was for. No one mentioned bringing the cover. I felt let down and hoped no one knew it was the oatmeal box I brought.

. . .

IN ANOTHER PAGE of this chapter of memories, my classmates and I were all sitting in a circle on the floor of the kindergarten room at the direction of the teacher. The room was well lit from the big windows to the east. There were blackboards on two sides of the room with the alphabet, both uppercase and lowercase, displayed above them. The desks were in rows in the front half of the room, but we were not using them for now. The teacher was there, and I was vaguely aware there were two other adults in the room. We were participating in an activity.

"Boys and girls, we are going to talk about the importance of eating breakfast. Breakfast gives you energy for the day. Let's go around the circle, and each of you can tell what you had for breakfast this morning. Let's start with you, Lois. What did you have for breakfast this morning?"

"Oatmeal."

"Okay. Next."

"Corn flakes."

"Bacon and eggs."

"Wheaties."

It was my turn, and I was silent, not sure what to say.

"Barbara, you are next. What did you have for breakfast this morning?"

"I didn't have any breakfast."

It was as if an alarm had gone off! It was as if they found what they had come for. As I look back now, it seems to me that maybe the extra adults in the room were part of a government program to find underprivileged, food-deprived children. There was some buzzing between them. They had success—except that they didn't uncover the reason I didn't eat breakfast. Truthfully, my mother tried to coax me into eating something, but I had a nervous stomach and refused to eat anything before I left for school.

After the completion of the sharing time around the circle, there were lectures on how important it is to eat breakfast. I felt shamed by the activity but was not converted.

A few weeks later, we apparently had the follow-up session. There we were. Same routine: sit on the floor in a circle and tell what we had for breakfast. Except that this time I lied. When it was my turn, I said:

"I had bacon and eggs for breakfast."

The adults exchanged knowing looks. They remembered me and had succeeded in their campaign to teach children to eat breakfast. Or maybe they succeeded in teaching one little girl to fabricate the truth.

I HAVE a hunch that we were part of yet another social services program: this one to make sure every kindergartner received at least one Christmas gift in this depression era. Someone, not the teacher, quizzed each student, "What do you want Santa to bring you for Christmas?" The expected answer for girls was "a doll."

I answered, "Blue and white dishes."

"Don't you want a doll?"

"No. I have a doll. I want blue and white dishes."

I received a disapproving look as she moved on to the next interview.

Santa Claus showed up on the last day of school before Christmas vacation. He was fat and jolly and dressed in his red and white fur-trimmed suit, saying, "Ho, Ho, Ho" as he walked up and down between the rows of desks. He drew gifts out of his bag, one by one, and every girl received a doll, and every boy received a toy truck from Santa. No matter what we asked for, we received the standard stereotyped gift.

I can't find any evidence as I check the internet that this was a government program, but in retrospect, it certainly felt like it. Or maybe it was a local social services program. Not that I couldn't find it within me to take care of another doll. It just didn't fill a need for me, but it was a nice gesture. Thank you, FDR, or whoever was responsible.

I never did get those blue and white dishes as a child, but I did buy my own blue and white Rosenthal China in Germany while on a grand tour of Europe in 1957 after I had taught school a few years. At that time, many young women purchased china or sterling silver for a "hope chest." I had never thought I wanted fine china. I was more of a pottery person. But when I saw the white china with a delicate blue edge, I fell in love with it. Immediately I thought, "It's my blue and white dishes!" I use them often.

Forgetting the oatmeal box lid. Saying the wrong thing when asked what I ate for breakfast. Wishes for blue and white dishes going unheeded. As I write, I wonder why negative experiences are so indelibly etched in my memory. I research the internet for clues. An expert says that recalling bad experiences is like re-living them, and each time the experience is re-lived, it burns the emotions, the shame, deeper into the memory. Forgiving oneself and letting go is a healthier way to deal with it.

AT AGE FIVE, I was also my mother's little errand girl, eager to do some special task, maybe typical of a middle child who developed into a pleaser looking for attention and approval. One errand that I recall was to go to the home of Mrs. Peterson, the Avon lady, and to bring home—not Avon products, which would have been lotions and perfumes, unheard of luxuries for us—but to have her fill the clean syrup pail I brought along with goat's milk from her pet goats. Goat's milk is rich and nutritious. My mother used it in cooking, and it must have been a bargain, or we would not have purchased it. The route to Mrs. Peterson's house was up the block, across the street, walk a block and a half, and turn left into the alley and walk one more block. I ran fast even in the winter time with the milk sloshing in the tightly covered pail, trying to impress my mother with my speed and efficiency.

One of my favorite errands was to deliver the $25 monthly rent check to our landlord, Mrs. Blaskey. They lived two houses north of us in what I thought was a grand house. It was on a corner lot next to the schoolhouse, white stucco with blue trim. A large window with colored, leaded glass at the top looked onto the front porch, which had cement railings wide enough to sit on. Grapevines, with leaves moving gently in the breeze, gave an airy feeling as they partially filled the opening on the north side, between the cement railing and the roof, looking towards the school.

I would go up the steps onto the blue-grey wooden porch and ring the doorbell. Soon Mrs. Blaskey would open the heavy, wooden door with the beveled glass inserts, and I would peek in just a little as I handed her the check. Little did I know then that seven years and three houses later that house would become an important part of our lives.

MY EARLY VENTURES into the world outside my home brought me in touch with people who were gentle and kind, such as my Sunday School teacher, people who were gruff and strict, such as the Sunday School superintendent, bullies who were mean and frightening, and lots of people in between, who were mostly matter of fact and business like. I was ready for more.

II

THE FRONT DOOR
HALF HOUSE

8

THE FRONT DOOR HALF HOUSE

WE BECAME THE FRONT DOOR HALF HOUSE PEOPLE WHEN the Kimballs found other housing and moved out. The main advantage of moving to the front side was the indoor plumbing. Now we had a bathroom with a flush toilet and claw-footed bathtub upstairs. And we had three bedrooms instead of one, which was appropriate for a family with three children.

Our main living room/dining room/kitchen all combined was on the ground floor and was accessed by the front door, which had a decorative frosted trim bordering the glass in the window in the upper half of the door. The window was attractive, but it didn't allow us privacy.

My main recollection of that door with the window was seeing a scruffy appearing, long-bearded hobo through the glass, as he persistently knocked on the door, hoping for a handout. I was frightened, but my mother calmly answered the door and sent him away with some potatoes. I had overheard adult conversation mentioning that houses were marked in some way by hobos for the benefit of other hobos—indicating whether or not it was likely they would receive a handout from this house. I looked around outside, but not knowing what to look for, couldn't see any markings on our house. I never thought of us as being poor—poor people were asking us for food, and we shared with them. This was clear evidence to me that we were not poor.

As WE ENTERED that front door, there was a wall to the immediate left which divided the main floor. The archway on that wall between the original living room and dining room was filled in with plywood and divided the furnace grate that we shared with the back-door people. Now we were on the other side and using the other half of the furnace grate!

Today it would be most unusual to bring one's kitchen along to a new rental place, but that is what we did in every house we rented and even to the house we finally bought. Our large cooking range, the stand-alone cupboard, and the icebox were moved from the back half of the house to the space across the room from the front door. We moved everything but the kitchen sink. In the far right corner, a sink was already hanging on the wall of the makeshift kitchen. The white enamel-topped table, an assortment of chairs, and the fold-out daybed completed the furniture in this multi-purpose room.

As we opened the front door, straight ahead against the back wall was the stairway, with three stairs up to a square landing and then eight stairs up to the right and turning again, three more stairs, with the three bedrooms and the bathroom doors all coming off a long hallway. It was luxurious to have more sleeping space.

Our parents acquired two more bedsprings and mattresses to furnish the bedrooms upstairs. Of course, they had their beautiful four-piece matching bedroom set with the waterfall front that my mother had purchased for $39. Sixty-four years later, when Mother moved into the nursing home at age 96, that bedroom set sold for $135, after giving her a lifetime of pleasure. I was thankful that she never asked who bought it, because it is highly unlikely that she would have approved of their occupation. She never knew that the new owners of her prized possession were the operators of the new Tattoo Parlor on Main Street.

Betty recalls that we did not use the bathtub very much. I suppose the tradition of a once-a-week bath remained with us, and we probably shared the bathwater as in the past. Frugal ways did not change much because frugality was what kept us within budget.

.   .   .

I NEVER QUESTIONED much of anything. I didn't know what other people did because I was not in their homes. And what we read in our textbooks about bathing every day was for the characters in the books and, unfortunately, I thought it had nothing to do with us. Just like our readers in first grade had no connection with us:

"Jane. See Jane. See Jane run. Run, Jane. Run.

Dick. See Dick. See Dick run. Run, Dick. Run."

The pictures of the parents in our readers did not look like our parents. The dad carried a briefcase and wore a suit. The mother had high heels. So our early readers in school taught us to read, but they did not teach us anything about everyday life. Unfortunately, it was a total disconnect in my mind.

ONE OF MY biggest memories from the Front Door Half House was that I had measles that year and spent time in an upstairs bedroom, alone quite a bit for a week or more, running a high fever. I remember it as a lonely time. In the Back Door Half House, we were accustomed to sleeping in the living room on a foldout daybed, which would have been in the midst of family activity. Now I was alone in a sparsely furnished, darkened upstairs bedroom.

Measles was considered a part of childhood. Sometimes parents deliberately exposed their children to measles and chickenpox, thinking they may as well get it over with and develop immunity. The measles vaccine was developed in 1963, the year my youngest child was born. Widespread use came a little later. As I write now in 2019, there are measles cases in the news again, and people who refuse to vaccinate are blamed for the outbreak.

When I was in my thirties, struggling with arthritis, a doctor noted that one of my hips was noticeably higher than the other, and he asked if I had had a high fever as a child during a growth period. Yes, measles. For the most part, there were no lasting effects from measles, but there were occasional deaths when it turned into encephalitis.

My sister Pat remembered that my dad had measles at the same time I did. He was in another bedroom upstairs, so Mother had two patients at the same time. We just let Nature take her course. Eventually, we would get well. No need to confer with a doctor over the measles. I must have had them during summer vacation because I do not remember missing school, and no one could go to school with a case of measles – not even me.

I prided myself on perfect attendance year after year and went to school even when I was not 100 percent well. I recall begging my Mother to let me go to school when I had a bad sore throat. She gave in, telling me I could go if I wore Dad's wool stocking with Vicks Vapor-rub on it, wrapped around my throat, thinking that would surely keep me home. But it didn't. I went to school wearing the stocking and smelling of Vicks. I think I had perfect attendance records nine of out of thirteen years (counting kindergarten). I really loved school! Or I loved the recognition of achieving perfect attendance.

I HAVE no recollection as to who lived in the back door side of the house when we moved to the front door side. Maybe it was empty. We still played in the whole yard, but now we had more access to the front porch. I remember jumping off the wide cement railings onto the ground, a distance of maybe five feet. Maybe that is why I have fallen arches.

That reminds me of the store where we purchased shoes and other merchandise: The Johnson Sisters Department Store on Main Street in Mahnomen. The store was owned and operated by a well-dressed Mr. Johnson, and his spinster sisters, also Johnsons. There was a most unusual collection of goods in that store: bolts and bolts of colorful satin fabric standing on end on a counter running down the center aisle, with price per yard written in pencil on the flat cardboard around which the fabric was wound. One could wonder why there was so much fancy fabric in a small town in depressed times. Waist-high glass cabinets lined the front and both sides of the center section, filled with items the customers had to ask to see.

Shoes and boots were in the back of the store, along with men's and women's clothing, and underwear for all. My mother accompanied me to the Johnson Sisters store to buy shoes. No sneakers were available in those days. We bought whatever fit—there were no out of town trips to shop. My feet were long and narrow and difficult to fit, so invariably I would end up with ugly leather oxford shoes with one-inch heels, totally undesirable for a young girl even in those days. They were probably expensive also, which would have been hard on mother's budget, but oh how I hated those shoes!

❦ 9 ❦

UNFAMILIAR TERRITORY

WHEN MY PARENTS MOVED US FROM TWIN VALLEY TO Mahnomen, Minnesota in 1934 when a job opened up for my dad, they were moving into unfamiliar territory. I sensed my mother had some hesitation about it. For her, this was probably not an adventure. Both of them were born in rural Ulen of parents who had emigrated from Norway. Ulen, and the town where they rented their first house, Twin Valley, were basically Scandinavian, Lutheran communities, where people tended to look alike, think alike, act alike, and sound alike, sharing the same Scandinavian accent. Many of them continued to speak Norwegian.

Mahnomen, however, was inside the boundaries of the White Earth Indian Reservation and was settled by people of more varied backgrounds, including Bohemians and Germans, and many of them were Catholic. There was a

Catholic grade school about two blocks from our house. There was also a convent, and we often saw the nuns in their black and white habits walking energetically on the sidewalk past our house in twos or threes, smiling and chatting with each other, with their rosaries and keys dangling as they moved. Their destination was the hospital at the north end of town where they worked.

Mahnomen was the county seat and the home of the courthouse. While Mahnomen was designated as Indian reservation territory, the Ojibway Indians tended to live by the lakes, twenty or more miles away from town and had their own settlements there. There was a part-Indian family living across the street from us in the corner house, a family with three big boys and a mother who hollered at them. They were the bullies we feared. We were not aware of many other Indians living in town, but we did see them going in and out of the places where they could buy beer: the Red Apple Cafe, the Corner Café, and the pool hall, sometimes in a drunken state. Because of that association, we did not hold them in high regard, an attitude we must have absorbed from our parents. We knew that for us to marry a Catholic was not desirable, but to date an Indian was not even to be considered. So we grew up with prejudice and didn't recognize that until much later. Prejudice is an ugly attitude that separates people from really knowing one another.

Our parents seemed hesitant in learning to trust their new environment and making connections with neighbors, but we did have visits from family. My parents' best friends were my dad's sister, Berniece, and her husband Richard Nielsen, an immigrant from Denmark. They lived in Ada, Minnesota, about 28 miles from Mahnomen, where Richard had a blacksmith shop, and Berniece was a teacher in a country school. It was from Uncle Richard we learned that the Danes were a superior people. He said so, and we believed it. He was tall and handsome and had a charming Danish accent. He was a storyteller, and his jokes were funny only because of the way he told them. And the number of times he told them with variations.

"A man went into a coffee shop. The
waitress asked him for his order.
'I'll have a cup of coffee and a donut.'
'I'm sorry, but we don't have any
donuts.'
'Okay. I will have a glass of milk and
a donut.'
'I'm sorry, sir, but we don't have any
donuts.'
'Okay. Well, just give me the donut.'

Uncle Richard laughed uproariously at his own jokes, and we all joined in. He was delightful.

Berniece and Richard and their children, Maren and Dick, were visitors in our home, and we in theirs, especially at holiday times: Thanksgiving, Christmas, Easter. They had double-dated with our parents before they were married.

Richard had emigrated from Denmark and was sponsored by Søren Jensen, who lived in Ulen, Minnesota, and that is how he became acquainted with Berniece. We loved hearing him tell his stories and sing his goofy songs over and over. His own children laughed and kind of rolled their eyes, but Berniece laughed and looked lovingly at him even though she must have heard these stories again and again. It was obvious that Berniece adored him. We had not seen such love before. Our parents got along all right, but they did not look adoringly at each other.

The Nielsens: Uncle Richard and Aunt Berniece, along with cousin Dick and cousin Maren

IT WAS NOT an easy move for my parents to begin with, but we were settling in. Although they didn't spend time much with friends, just having Uncle Richard and Aunt Berniece come for a visit made our house feel cozy. To me, it was home. Then one day I was surprised to learn we were moving again, this time to the other end of town.

III

THE HOUSE UP NORTH

❧ 10 ❧

THE HOUSE UP NORTH

W E REFERRED TO OUR NEXT home as "The House Up North" for obvious reasons: it was in the north end of town. Actually, it was only eight blocks from where we were living in the Half House rental, and six blocks from the school, which seemed to be the center of our lives. Once again, we became Back Door People. We had a nice front door with cement steps and a railing, but it seems to me we only used it for taking pictures.

Betty and me in front of The House Up North

The rest of the time, we were always in and out of the back door.

As soon as I learned to read, I pictured the setting for the stories I read in locations I had already visited. The House Up North was the unlikely setting for many stories for me, even as I grew older. Even into my sixties and seventies, I was picturing stories set in that humble location: the queen of England's kitchen, staffed with servants; the prison for the misunderstood Christian mystic Jeanne Guyon, etc. No matter how vivid, the author's descriptions could not override my imagination or what I had experienced.

The House Up North was a small stucco bungalow on a corner lot, facing south, bordered by an alley and two name-less streets. A large oak tree dominated the yard between the house and the alley, providing shade, a branch for a tire swing, and of course, a place to climb.

That oak tree also became the headquarters for our pretend circus. We saved our meager allowance money all year for two big occasions—Christmas and treats and rides at the Mahnomen County Fair in July. The fair had free admission to the grandstand to see the show, which included trapeze artists, tight-rope walkers, and circus animals. We often "played circus," inspired by our time at the fair. We tried to make a tight-rope, with one end tied around the big tree in the yard, and the other end onto whatever seemed strong enough to hold our weight, but we couldn't ever seem to get it taut enough. Even our building attempts were part of our play. We involved neighborhood children and did showman antics with some of us doing the acting and some being the audience. We passed many hours, enjoying our performances and our failures.

Wherever we were, we always managed to make our own fun. Even the large shed out back next to the outhouse that was intended to serve as a garage or a toolshed or storage became for us a place to hide out and climb and play.

Walking to and from school from this house involved two hazards: a nippy Chow Chow dog named Chang who resembled a small lion with a golden mane, and a bully named Billy Z. (fictitious name to protect the guilty). The solution to avoiding the dog was simply to walk across the street because his chain limited his reach to sidewalk walkers. We just hoped the chain would hold. The bullies were not so easy to avoid. Billy Z., a heavy-set boy in overalls, was ready to chase us whenever his route paralleled ours. I discovered that I sometimes could pop into Roy's Garage and Machine Shop where Dad worked to hide out for a few minutes, if necessary. At the time, it was frightening. If we had called his bluff, he would perhaps have backed off. But Billy Z. remains a childhood memory. A negative one. I wonder if he is still living and what kind of life he has had.

OUR OLD FURNITURE once again found a new home in the House Up North, which was smaller than what we had become accustomed to: a kitchen, a dining room/living room, and one bedroom. No bathroom. So my sister Betty and I adjusted to sleeping on the daybed in the living room again. Little sister Patty probably shared our parents' bedroom. There was no room to eat in the kitchen, so our dining room table and chairs were again set up in the combined dining-living room. There was no big furnace to feed with coal or oil in this house, nor was there a metal furnace grate to stand on during cold wintery mornings. Instead, a metal space heater occupied the area just inside the dining room door—which sometimes became red-hot and dangerous to the touch.

The game I remember playing most (until our parents put a stop to it) was called "run around and catch each other." There were three of us. One would call out a challenge: "Bet you can't catch me!" to the others and then run from the kitchen, through the dining/living room, through the only bedroom and back into the kitchen. Because it was a circular route, it was difficult to tell who was chasing whom. I think it was during one of those games that little Patty fell against the red-hot metal space heater and got burned. But once again, the burns were treated at home, as were most of our illnesses or accidents.

The treadle sewing machine that followed us from house to house often served as a prop in our make-believe game called "hubby and wifey." Hubby was the breadwinner of the house, and he went off to work each day. His work involved operating the treadle of Mother's Singer sewing machine, pushing it up and down, imitating a factory job. Wifey said goodbye to him and busied herself in her make-believe kitchen.

Our magnificent stove with the four burners, warming ovens, and water reservoir took up a lot of the space in the kitchen, along with the wood box. Under the east window, there was a counter with a sink built into it and a hand pump that delivered water right inside the house. I'm not sure how the water drained since there was no indoor plumbing. My mother was amazing how she adjusted to all these varying circumstances, but as my sister Pat recently reminded me, she was used to similar conditions growing up, so maybe it felt like home. I wonder what advantage this house was for her—cheaper rent, very likely. And privacy probably—we were no longer under the same roof with strangers. It was nice to be in charge of our own space.

WE DIDN'T ALWAYS HAVE a storm cellar, but fortunately, we did at this house, because we actually used it for a storm. The double trap doors, weather-worn wide planks, about four feet by six feet, lay at an angle sloping from the foundation of the house to the ground. Metal rings on both doors provided a means of lifting the doors open to reveal cement stairs down into a basement. Windows provided a little bit of light in the basement.

The Year the Tornado Struck Mahnomen, a tornado tail formed below dark grey clouds on the horizon, and my parents quickly rounded us up to head for the cellar through those doors. The tornado did touch down on the countryside near Mahnomen but did not affect us in town. Later, my dad took us for a ride in the country to see what the force of a tornado could do—uproot huge trees, demolish a farm building and leave nearby buildings untouched, and even drive a straw through a glass windowpane. Unbelievable. I can still picture my dad in his familiar pin-striped overalls, leaning forward on the steering wheel of the car, driving ever so slowly on those country roads, looking from side to side at the devastation. Huge trees broken in half looked like something from another world. He was clearly impacted by the destruction which took many months of cleanup and years for the trees to grow back.

That same year was also the Year of the Grasshopper Invasion. Arriving in thick dark clouds, the slippery green grasshoppers covered the streets and sidewalks, making it difficult to walk. Our big garden was stripped bare by the hoard. That meant there would be no home-canned green beans, nor would there be a potato or carrot crop that winter. It was a blow to Mother's food budget, but a small problem for us compared to that of the farmers, whose crops were devoured, leaving bare sticks in the ground where the plants had grown. It was one more hardship for people struggling to make ends meet in the depression. When we talked about the plagues in the Old Testament story, I pictured those green grasshoppers covering the countryside.

I WASN'T conscious that we were poor, but it did register with me that we had more than some of our neighbors and less than others. We had more than the very poor family whose house had a cement floor and scarce furniture. I can't remember their names, but they were kind, welcoming people. Once the father in that home helped me carry home groceries when he was walking my way as I returned from an errand for my mother. We had much less than the people who lived in the impressive brick house that was kitty-corner the other way from us. "Law" Wilson lived there with his college-age son and his petite, well-dressed, bird-like wife. We never saw the inside of their house, and we never really knew them. We only saw them in church and coming and going from their garage.

Barb standing on the front steps of The House Up North

My first boyfriend (John Ederer), a fellow third-grader, was the son of the local doctor, and they lived across the street, east from the Wilsons. We bought their old refrigerator when they purchased a new one, which was a step up from our old icebox, which had to be furnished with blocks of ice to keep food cold.

I was in their house a few times when playing with John. My most vivid memory was the sparkling clean, modern kitchen, and the lemon pie sitting on the table. John had permission to eat the pie, but he wasn't interested. Of course, I did not eat it either since he was not interested, even though he offhandedly said, "you can have some." That was beyond comprehension for me—both the opportunity to eat lemon pie and the declining of it.

THE MYSTERY BOX FROM AUNT BERTHA

Lewis, Bertha and baby Berniece

M Y DAD HAD SEVEN BROTHERS and sisters, and I knew most of them: Oscar, George, Gina, Amanda, Bernice, and Clifford —probably because when they married, they never moved far away. But Aunt Bertha—she was a mystery person to me. She never married. She went out to Montana to work as a nanny for a well-to-do family, made a good life for herself, and rarely came home.

One day a box of used clothing from Montana arrived at the Braseth farm. It was from Aunt Bertha. It was a large box, maybe 3 ft by 3 ft by 3 ft high, loaded with dresses and shoes, sweaters and other used clothing, discards from the family she worked for, all packed together. We were invited to dig in and find a treasure or two to take home. I remember spying a pair of lace-up leather shoe boots, scuffed and worn, in need of polish, very old-fashioned looking. They looked interesting to me, so I asked my mother if I could have them.

"I suppose," she said.

I also chose a black, long-sleeved rayon dress that fit my slim nine-year old body. It was a princess-style coatdress and had eight large round brass buttons all down the front. I thought it was nice, so that also became one of the treasures I took home.

The next morning when I dressed for school, I asked if I could wear the boot shoes to school.

"If you want to, you can," said Mother.

I laced them up tight to make them fit and practiced walking in them. They worked, so I wore them to my fourth grade classroom. As I sat at my desk swinging my legs back and forth, I was suddenly aware they were not as desirable as I had thought. My classmate in the row across the aisle was staring at my unusual shoes. I had never been embarrassed about my own scuffed shoes, but I wanted to sit on these to cover them up. When I went home for lunch at noon, I took them off and put on my old shoes. I never wore those boots again.

The black princess style dress suffered a similar ending. I

happily wore it to church where Beverly Berge, a year older than me, a very pleasant person, commented on it. She said, "Did you get a new dress?"

I said, "My Grandma gave it to me." Which was close to the truth. I didn't want to say it came out of a box of hand-me-downs sent from Montana by my Aunt Bertha.

Beverly asked, "Was it hers?"

I was crushed. If it looked like a grandmother's dress, I surely did not want to wear it. I never wore that again, either. A recurring thought surfaced again—were we poor? Apparently Aunt Bertha thought so.

12

THE SHOPPING TRIP

"MY PARENTS SAID I COULD INVITE YOU ALONG ON OUR shopping trip to Fargo on Saturday. Do you want to come?" It was Solveig Stortroen, a classmate and friend from Sunday School, who extended the invitation. Her father, Albert Stortroen, was the pastor of First Lutheran Church. My parents didn't go to church all that often, so sometimes I went anyway and sat with Solveig. We were becoming good friends, and she had just invited me to her birthday party at the parsonage, which was two blocks northwest of the House Up North.

I wasn't sure what a shopping trip was. Do you mean people went to other towns and purchased a list of things they needed or wanted and came back with a lot of new stuff? My mother sewed my dresses, and our underwear, stockings, and shoes either came from the Johnson Sisters store on Main

Street in Mahnomen or from the catalog or from hand-me-downs. I asked my mother about it. She said I could go if I wanted to and that we would probably be eating in a restaurant if we would be away all day. She would give me money to pay for my lunch if that situation arose.

I told Solveig that yes, I did want to go. Her sister Valeria also took a friend along, and the four of us were in the back seat of the car for the 75-mile trip to Fargo, North Dakota. That was the first time I had ever been out of the state of Minnesota in my nine years of life.

I can't remember the shopping part at all, but I do remember that we ate lunch in a restaurant, the first time ever for me. The waitress asked each of us what we wanted. I'm quite sure I needed help in ordering, but I was pleased when the waitress placed a hamburger sandwich in front of me. When it was time to pay, Pastor Stortroen would not take my money, but generously paid the whole bill

First-time experiences serve as markers in our lives. Looking back, they become contrast points with the lives of our own children. We didn't eat out often when our children were growing up unless we were traveling. But by the time they were nine years old, in the late 1960s and early 1970s, they had traveled across the country to the East Coast, to the West Coast, and far south on extended camping trips in connection with their dad's advanced schooling. We had also lived in Oregon for a school year in 1967-68. Fast food restaurants were beginning to get established, and as we traveled, we had options to choose whether we wanted McDonald's,

Hardees, or Kentucky Fried Chicken for supper. At that time, it was a big treat for all of us.

Eric was only nine, Jenny was twelve, and Julie was fourteen when the family traveled to Europe in 1973 on a month-long trip, also connected with Harvey's teaching at Waldorf College. Quite a contrast when my biggest trip at age nine was 75 miles across the Minnesota border into North Dakota, and that at the generosity of friends. I did, indeed, lead a sheltered life.

Solveig continued to be a good friend for me over the next three years. I always felt comfortable in church activities because I could count on her being there. As the daughter of the pastor, she had to be there.

When we were in seventh grade, Pastor Stortroen announced to the congregation that he had accepted a call to a parish in Amery, Wisconsin, and they would be leaving Mahnomen in a few weeks. I was devastated by the news. I remember walking out early from the church-packed farewell meeting in tears, overwhelmed by my loss. Solveig would be making new friends, but I was experiencing a big hole in my life. Children can feel those losses deeply. I know I did.

❧ 13 ❧

BEST FRIENDS EVER

WHEN MY MOTHER WENT INTO THE MAHNOMEN NURSING Home as a resident when she was 96 years old, she was lonely and had a hard time adjusting. When asked how it was, she said, "If I just had a pal, it would be all right." Eventually one of the long-time friends she worked with in the school hot lunch program, Ellen Thompson, moved from a beautiful nursing home in Fargo back to the Mahnomen Nursing Home, and they both then had a pal.

We never outgrow our need for friends. We all need someone we enjoy being with, someone we can count on to be true to us whether we are together or apart, someone we connect with through interests or values.

Patsy Mattix was that kind of friend for me. In fact, we did so much together that I called her my best friend in grade school. She was a brown-eyed girl with freckles and rosy cheeks, a year younger than I. I can still remember the beautiful pink crocheted dress she wore on Sundays when she went with her parents to the Congregational church. Her mother had made it for her, and it was unlike any dress I had ever seen. As she grew, her mother could crochet more rows to lengthen the dress so it took years for her to grow out of it.

I am standing with Patsy Mattix (wearing her crocheted dress) on the front steps of the House Up North

The best thing about Patsy's attending the Congregational Church is that she got a Sunday School paper called What To Do, which was much more exciting than anything we received at the Lutheran Church. It was filled with

DS *and* **ONION**
EACH ONE PRINTED. SEND AS MANY AS YOU LIKE.
chool that   When I received my third W. T. D.
alize how   prize in three weeks, my dad asked me
ble paper.   if those crisp and crinkly $1 bills were
rnia.   counterfeit!—Barbara Braseth, Mahno-
wasting   men, Minnesota.
s. I said   If anybody asks me, I think W. T. D.
ng. Then   would be a better paper if it contained
u should   less P. L. and more jokes.—Sarajean

*One of my prize-winning entries that
was printed and generously rewarded*

puzzles that awarded one-dollar bill prizes for correct answers. She shared the papers with me, and we entered the contests and actually received crisp one-dollar bills as prize money ten or twelve times. I saved the envelopes with the WHAT TO DO return address long after I had spent the money. They are still in my scrapbook! It was outrageously exciting for me to receive a letter in the mail with money in it!

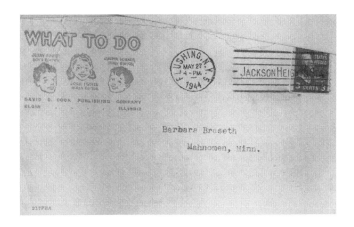

One of many envelopes saved in a scrapbook

"MISCHIEVOUS" is not a word that would normally describe me, but I do remember a prank that Patsy and I played one day: The country was coming out of the Great Depression and the government began creating jobs for people who had no other income. Between the years 1935 and 1943, the government sponsored work projects in Minnesota under the Works Progress Administration (WPA). Many projects involved building libraries and schools and installing water and sewer lines. One of those projects was to hand-dig trenches and lay water pipes in the alley between the Mattix house and one of their neighbors.

As Patsy and I ran back and forth between our houses, we noticed these men leaning on their shovels, taking a rest from the tiresome work in the heat of the day. We understood why some people said that WPA stood for "We Poke Along."

On one particular day we saw a muscular young worker enter the porta potty outhouse. I don't know what possessed us to do it, but after noticing there was a hook lock on the outside of the door, we sneaked up quietly and locked it, locking him in. The moment he discovered our mischievous deed, he banged on the door and shouted angrily at us. He guessed who was behind the prank. We ran and hid and watched as one of his co-workers rescued him. In the days ahead, we avoided the area, afraid of being found guilty and reprimanded.

I can't quite imagine that we had the audacity to do such

a thing because we were usually very obedient children. I am not condoning the prank, but it served for me to be a personal connection to the WPA from the Roosevelt administration in my growing up years. Without that incident seared into my memory, the WPA might have merely been a textbook fact to me.

Patsy and I were not only best friends, we were almost-neighbors in two neighborhoods. When I lived in the House Up North, she was just a couple of blocks away in a big two-story house that her parents were renting. To my dismay, they built a house and moved to the other side of town. But to my delight, our move to our next house (the Slukey House) would bring us close together again.

Patsy's dad was the manager of the Mahnomen Grain Elevator; and with that came the privilege of our being able to play there. Multiple railroad tracks laced the ground behind the elevator, with potential for switching cars close to the elevator for loading grain. We played in and around those railroad cars. Sometimes we played in the grain bins, slipping and sliding in the flax and corn in our bare feet until her dad put a stop to it. This could actually be dangerous. Once we explored the area along the railroad tracks behind the elevator and came upon hobos cooking their food over a campfire. Their scruffy beards and rough appearances were intimidating. We dared not go very close.

To go swimming in the summertime, sometimes we walked on the railroad tracks through neighborhoods of houses and eventually came to a train trestle high above the

dam area in the park where we could swim. Walking across
the tracks on the trestle above the dam was risky unless one
was sure of the train schedule. One could not outrun the train
once it was within hearing distance. It was not a safe activity
for us, but the big boys did it regularly. If we heard the train
whistle while we were swimming in the area down below, we
all looked up to watch the train rumble across the trestle, to
wave at the engineer, and to see if there was anyone on the
trestle. I recall seeing the big boys hanging on the outer edge
of the wooden framework that supported the tracks while the
train rumbled on the track just inches away. I can't imagine
the strength it would take to hang on. A fall would land them
in the water below the dam.

River scene, Mahnomen Minnesota, 1910's. Courtesy LakesnWoods.com
Postcard and Postcard Image Collection

The swim area was near the dam which was directly

under the trestle and had dangerous undercurrents that could pull a swimmer under the water. We stayed away from the area where the water pooled under the dam and didn't go in the water unless there was a lifeguard on duty. We could wear our swim suits under our clothes for the walk to the river or change in the public outhouse, but we took a chance at having our clothes (at least our underwear) stolen while in the water. It was not like the controlled pool areas of today! I'm not sure our parents had a clear picture of the whole situation. They always gave us permission to go swimming.

Raking with Patsy

WE OFTEN TALK about where we were when we first heard about significant historical events. I was ten years old when I first heard about the events that would draw our country once again into a World War. I spent a lot of time over at the new Mattix house, and I was in their kitchen with Patsy on December 7, 1941, when the news came over the radio that the Japanese had bombed Pearl Harbor. Mrs. Mattix, who was a little older than my mother, a full-bosomed, well-corseted lady with quick movements, a stream of chatter, and a kind heart, was very upset. I couldn't figure out how that could impact us because the Hawaiian Islands were so very far away. But Patsy had two older brothers who were of an age that they would be drafted into the armed services. I began to understand in a more experiential way that a war in a faraway place could actually affect our lives in Mahnomen, Minnesota.

CHILDHOOD FRIENDS ARE an important part of our most formative years. It's easy to lose touch, and they remain only as fond memories in our lives. The Mattix's moved to North Dakota to manage another grain elevator when Patsy started high school so that separation broke our ties for many years. But we reconnected later in life, continued to exchange Christmas cards, and are still friends to this day. Good friends are a matchless blessing!

IV

THE SLUKEY HOUSE

❧ 14 ❧

THE SLUKEY HOUSE

IN 1941, WHEN I WAS IN FIFTH GRADE, WE MOVED TO THE
Slukey house, so named because that was the name of our
landlord. In one way it seemed like we were regressing. It had
been two houses ago that we last had an indoor bathroom,
and we had just gotten used to running water in the kitchen in
The House Up North. The Slukey House had neither
running water nor an indoor toilet, but as I look back on those
two years we lived there, I would never have imagined so
many great things would happen.

The Slukey house was two blocks east of the school building, on a corner lot facing east, so it was an easy walk to
school. A mustard-colored, two-story wooden frame house
with a front porch that had white spindle rails, it had a front
door with a frosted glass window, an entrance which we never
used. Again, we became Back Door People, even though we

had the whole house. I can't explain it. It wasn't that we were keeping the front entrance for guests because we never had any guests. Maybe it was because the front door was never in the direction we were going. The back door was just closer to everything that was important: school, uptown, and our friends.

Getting my 11th birthday picture in front of the Slukey House

Across the street from our front door stood a tired old gas station with one gas pump, no longer in service. North of that, the large weathered grain elevator where Patsy and I played stood as a peak in the Mahnomen skyline that could be recognized from a distance away.

Our back porch was not only our main entrance, but it was an important part of our house. Whenever someone came into our house, they would have to walk by the hand pump, the piles of wood stacked against the wall, and the Maytag wringer washing machine that was stored when it was not in use. That porch description sounds so trashy when I think about it now, but I don't remember being embarrassed about it at the time. It just was what it was. We needed a place for those things and the back porch served the purpose.

Every ounce of water that came into the house came out of that hand pump, whether it was for drinking water or cooking or baths or washing clothes.

My dad chopped the wood and stacked it on the porch, and it was my job to keep the wood box by the kitchen stove full. I tried to do it without being reminded, because I knew it would please my mother, and that erased the negative feelings associated with chores.

Our Maytag wringer washing machine was brought into the kitchen for the weekly laundry routine. What a lot of work that was for my mother! The water had to be pumped on the porch and carried in, heated on the stove in a 20 inch by 13 inch by 12 inch copper boiler, and then dipped into the washing machine. My dad helped with that before he left for work the morning of washday. Mother shaved her laundry soap, which was Fels Naptha bar soap, into the washing machine water, filled the two rinse tubs with warm or cold water, sorted the clothes, washing the whites first, then the coloreds, then the greasy overalls, all taking turns in the same water. The washer made a rhythmic noise as it swished the clothes first one direction and then back again, chugging relentlessly against the weight of the wet clothes. Each load had to be put through the wringer into the rinse rubs, first one and then the other, and finally put through the wringer again to get the excess water out.

1931 Maytag wringer washer. From "Evolution of the Maytag Washer," www.maytagclub.com

Sometimes I helped, folding buckles and buttons inside the clothes so they didn't get caught between the wringer rollers, being careful not to let my fingers get pulled into the wringer along with the garments. Then we carried the heavy basket full of wet clean clothes to the clothesline alongside the garden in the back yard, pinning them to the wire line with wooden clothespins. In the winter the clothes were put on folding wooden racks and set outside on the porch to freeze and then brought into the dining room to dry out. None of us enjoyed the wet clothes hanging around but the moisture was likely good for the humidity level. It was all part of the washday routine.

Of course that Maytag wringer washing machine went with us when we moved. Much later my mother was offered her sister's modern washing machine that used all clean water for every wash load and rinse load. It was hard for my mother to see that little-used water gushing down the drain pipes, so my dad set up a system to save the water and use it for the next load. This "suds saver" was never satisfactory. Mother reverted back to using the old-fashioned washer with tubs and wringer long after she needed to. The waste of water was abhorrent to her, even when she no longer had to pump it or pay extra for using more.

THE KITCHEN FURNISHINGS were really familiar because they came with us each time we moved. But since we didn't have running water, there was something new to this house. As we entered the kitchen, to the left there was a washstand with a chipped white enamel wash dish for washing hands and face, and brushing teeth (and shaving for Dad) and beyond that a place for drinking water, including a dipper in a crock. This washstand was reminiscent of the one in my mother's childhood home, so perhaps it didn't seem like a hardship to her. The rent for this house was $17 a month, $8 less than the $25 a month we paid for our first rental. Mother made a game out of being thrifty, stashing away money for the future, so perhaps the inconveniences she endured made it worthwhile for her.

Wedged into the corner along that same wall was the wood box and at a right angle stood the grand wood-burning cook stove with the claw feet and warming ovens up above and the water reservoir at the end. The stand-alone cupboard claimed the corner space, and the white metal-topped table hugged the wall under the window to the north, looking out on the garden and beyond that, the blacksmith shop. It was used mostly for breakfast and for a working space for mother's cooking and baking preparations. Next to the table stood a tall olive green tin cupboard for storage of canned goods, and beyond that there was a door to a pantry with shelves for storing food supplies—and next to that the second-hand refrigerator.

The most unique thing to me was the trapdoor to the cellar in the middle of the kitchen floor. There was a four-inch metal ring for a handle that lay flat in a track on the floor so we wouldn't trip over it, to be used to raise up the door when we needed to access the cellar. The cellar may have been intended for a storm retreat but I don't recall any such emergency during the two years we lived here. We used it for storing root vegetables harvested from our garden, such as potatoes and carrots, over the winter.

The dining room was the setting for our table and chairs and we regularly ate our meals there on the oil-cloth covered table. I recall the decorative wooden radio sitting on a shelf up high, and hearing the calming voice of President Franklin Delano Roosevelt reassuring us that everything would be all right even though we were at war. We also listened to the soap opera "Old Ma Perkins" as we ate lunch each day, having walked home from school. Beyond the dining room was another room furnished with our old daybed with the sagging springs that used to be our bed where Mother sometimes took a much-deserved nap, a black spindle rocking chair with a high back, and eventually a piano.

The stairway to the second floor originated from the dining room and as we climbed the stairs to the bedroom area, we could look through the spindle railings and see the rounded, enamel chamber pot with the white lid hiding under the bed for nighttime potty use. The two bedrooms led from one into the other without a hallway. My parents had the farthest one so we wouldn't be traipsing through their private quarters.

Our bedroom had two beds for three girls, so two had to share. We drew an imaginary line down the middle, each forbidding the bed partner to ever cross that line. Heavy homemade quilts served as covers and bedspreads. We played library in this room, assembling all the books we could find. We "accessioned" them, pasting old Sunday school offering envelopes in the back of the books to hold the check-out cards. With my 10 cents a week allowance, I bought a stamp set with letters and numbers at the dime store, and used it to stamp the due date. I don't think we had any customers outside our family and would never have let our books out into the neighborhood anyway. Imaginary library customers worked just fine.

Patty, Betty, me, and of course, Boots

OUR BLACK AND white short-haired dog named Boots shared this house with us. A rat terrier, very smart, she could hear the opening of a cookie jar from anywhere in the house and appear quickly, wagging her stub of a tail. Boots had several litters of pups and when it was time to deliver, she made a nest and hid away in the closet we shared between rooms, presenting us with a litter of three or four furry little crea-tures. Oh how we loved playing with those pups! We dressed them in doll clothes and pushed them in our doll carriage. I especially cared about the one with a crooked tail. But of course, we had to find another home for them when they were weaned from their mother. It was a sad day when we had to say goodbye to "Broken Tail" and his siblings.

A ONE-STALL CAR garage bordered the property on the west side of our house, and behind that a two-hole outhouse with a moon crest cut near the top into the door for ventilation and light. At the back corner of the property stood a storage shed with straw on the floor that looked like it had been built to house an animal, with separation stalls within the building. My dad used it to store our winter supply of wood for the cook stove, but we also played in that building and climbed on top of it, imagining it to be many things, including a store where we sold items to each other or a lookout for a game of cowboys and Indians.

There were several oak trees on the property, so we had good shade and a not-so-good lawn. Considering we threw our dirty water out the back door (no indoor plumbing), and with all the neighborhood kids playing there, it would have been challenging to grow grass anyway.

Our yard was a magnet for the neighborhood kids for playing games in the evenings. We played Ante-I-Over with two teams, throwing a ball over the house or the garage. If a team member caught the ball without it touching the ground, everyone ran around to the other side of the house to tag the other team.

An even more popular game was Hit the Tin Can Off. You can tell by the name of the game it didn't require sophisticated equipment. One team player hits an empty tin can off a tree stump using a stick, and in the time it takes for him to retrieve it and replace it on the stump, everyone runs and hides. The "hiders" sneak back to the stump and yell "FREE," while the hitter tries to tag someone to be "it" for the next round. Such great exercise and camaraderie! Kids from other neighborhoods joined in as we played under the streetlight those summer nights until we were called in by Mother: "It is time to quit. Come in. Bedtime." And everyone reluctantly scattered.

My 11th birthday party with my girlfriends and sisters: Patsy Mattix, Betty, Mary Francis Rumreich, Barb, Mary Kathryn Whiting, and Patty (by the back door of the Slukey House)

Just beyond our vegetable garden on the North side of the house stood a blacksmith shop, with the sagging double doors standing open to the street, revealing a fiery furnace that changed metal into white-hot shapes at the direction of the blacksmith. Sometimes we just stood and watched as Carl the blacksmith pulled the white-hot horseshoe out of the fire and hammered it, plunging it into a barrel of cold water to set the shape.

A young boy, age 9 or 10, Richard Garvey, one of the many who played games with us in the evenings, sometimes walked through our yard, and hung around the blacksmith shop, watching the blacksmith through the open doors. He often ate a whole package of six frosted sweet rolls which could be purchased at the grocery store for five cents from the day-old shelf. Mother, kneading bread dough on the table by the window, noticed him, and made the comment, partly to herself and partly to whoever was listening: "Those Garvey kids are hungry."

Her comment made me think about our life. I felt secure and happy in our home, well cared for. Mother kept the house clean and tidy and served us three meals a day. I never went hungry. (Well, not for long, that is. After school we were starved and wolfed down half a loaf of bread with jelly). We had freedom to read and to play, to spend time with friends indoors and outdoors. We went ice skating at the local outdoor ice rink, less than two blocks away, night after night, or sledding on the big hill above the river on Saturdays during the winter, and swimming in the water that pooled and gushed below the dam on the Wild Rice River in the summer. We played at our friends' homes or in our home. There were no organized sports or activities but we rarely lacked for something to do. Life in the Slukey house was never boring. It was all that I needed as an eleven-year-old. Except a bike. And a piano. And a baby brother. And we were soon to acquire all three.

15

THE BLUE AND WHITE BICYCLE

"BARB, WILL YOU RUN DOWN TO THE HARTZ STORE AND GET A can of white chunk tuna so I can make tuna casserole?" It was mid-afternoon and Mother was resting on the daybed in the living room, her house all tidy. She was formulating her last-minute supper menu and added: "Ask them to put it on my bill."

I was assembling a much-used interlocking picture puzzle on the dining room table, but didn't mind the interruption.

"Save the puzzle for me till I get back." I was off and running, letting the screen door slam behind me, *thud, thud, thud* down the wooden back porch steps and out into the street. I liked doing these errands. When I got to the end of the block, I was on Main Street. Turning right, I crossed the street and walked past the new stone Liquor Store/ Library/ Fire Station recently built by the Works Progress Administra-

tion. We used the library so often, we felt we had part owner-
ship in it.

I crossed the side street, went past the movie theatre to the
end of the block and halfway into the next block, and arrived
at the L.B.Hartz Grocery. Today's specials were painted on
the inside of the glass windows. "Quite a feat," I thought, "to
paint letters backwards." Up three steps and into the store, I
asked the clerk behind the counter for the tuna fish. He left
his position at the cash register, went to the lone aisle to the
right, and retrieved it from the six-foot high shelf of canned
goods. The small-town grocery stores were not self-service. He
wrote the purchase down in the ledger with our family name
on it and simply expected my mother to come in and pay her
bill on Saturday night.

With my purchase in hand, I headed home, crossing the
street at the bank corner. When I walked past the Coast to
Coast Store, I spotted it--the blue and white bicycle in the
window. The price tag clearly said $22.95, a sum totally out
of reach for me. I stood and stared at it. It was love at first
sight, and I was wondering already how I could make that
bike my own.

At suppertime, as our family of five was sitting around the
dining room table enjoying the tuna casserole, I told my
parents about the bike, and it became a topic of family
interest.

My dad raised the question, "How are you going pay
for it?"

"Maybe I could save the money," I said weakly, even

though it looked like an impossible task.

My sisters agreed it would be great to own that bike.

"Maybe we could all help pay for it and share the bike," Betty said.

After a little more discussion, my dad made a proposal. Patty and I could save $10 together in my cash register bank, Betty could contribute $5, Mother could add $5 from the grocery money, and when we had the $20, my dad would put in the remaining $2.95. It sounded like a workable plan.

My cash register bank was a cherished birthday present, a toy metal version of a steel cash register, colorfully decorated in curlicue designs in red, yellow and black paint. When coins (nickels, dimes and quarters) were inserted into the slot, it would register the amount deposited and update the total amount contained in the bank. The instructions that came with the bank promised that when the total registered $10, the door on the side of the bank would automatically open. That seemed like magic to me.

The year was 1942 and Patty was only seven, I was eleven, and Betty was thirteen. Our earning powers differed, so it was understood that I would be contributing more than Patty as we filled the bank together. Feeling very big sisterly and happy that we had a plan for getting the bike, I was perfectly okay with that.

The question was how we were going to earn the money. Our allowances by this time were 15 cents a week. A child's movie ticket sold for nine cents for a Sunday afternoon matinee. The theatre owner and manager, Charlie Vondra, a tall,

well-dressed gentleman, was engaging in the universal practice of trying to pay the least tax possible. Federal taxes were
collected on all tickets priced 10 cents and higher, so he
passed along the savings to his young customers (My source of
this inside information is from one of my sisters, both of
whom at some time sold tickets at the theatre.)

Rainbow Theatre, Mahnomen Minnesota, 1930's. Courtesy
LakesnWoods.com Postcard and Postcard Image Collection

So with my 15 cents allowance, I could go to the movie for
nine cents and buy a treat for a nickel—either popcorn at the
theatre or a triple ice cream cone later at the ice cream shop
—and have a penny left over. Or I could buy an apple, an
orange, and a banana for the nickel when shopping with
Mother at the grocery store. Or I could put it in the cash
register bank for the purchase of the bike. Truly this was a
lesson in delayed gratification.

Another way to earn money was to babysit. I hated
babysitting, especially for the family who lived across the

street. Their house was a mess, the children were dirty (as were their diapers), and I didn't know how to make order out of chaos. Nor did I want to. My mother kept our house very clean and orderly, and I wasn't required to help much, so I didn't have much experience. However, my dad frowned on turning down an opportunity to earn money, and I thrived on approval and wilted under disapproval, so I usually felt compelled to take the job when asked. The parents often stayed out way past midnight, and we had no way to reach them if we had trouble because we didn't have telephones. And for all this my pay averaged a nickel an hour.

Besides the money I earned from babysitting, we also managed to get a few coins from gathering recycled materials. Our country was at war and that meant certain commodities were rationed. It also meant that there was a new emphasis on recycling. Even the aluminum foil around individual sticks of gum and the foil lining of cigarette packages were items that could be collected and recycled. We rarely bought gum and no one that we knew smoked cigarettes, but we would look for discarded gum wrappers and cigarette packages on the street and formed the foil into a ball of aluminum. When it reached the required size, we could turn it in for a few pennies. It all helped towards the war effort and getting the cash register bank to register the magic number of $10.

I had one more unusual way to earn some money, and it was all because I was friends with Patsy Mattix, the best friend ever. Mr. Mattix, a kind, businesslike man with round, wire-framed eyeglasses, resembling Harry S. Truman in his demeanor and posture, brought home from the elevator some bags of rye grain that had a fungus growing on the grain. The fungus was called "ergot" and had some medicinal value. The Mattix family would sit around a card table in the evenings and "pick ergot," separating it from the grain using tweezers. The ergot was about the size of a grain of rice, and a two-ounce cup of ergot would be worth 50 cents, an amazing amount of money to me. Several times they invited me to join them in picking ergot and readily paid me on the spot when I had filled my two-ounce cup. My sister says she remembers being jealous that I got to pick ergot.

Recently I discovered that the ergot was poisonous if ingested, and if it had been left in the grain and ground up and used for flour to make bread, it would have made those who ate it very sick. I wonder how many rye bread lovers fell mysteriously ill and never knew why.

At the same time we were saving for the bike, the government launched an advertising campaign for children to invest in the war effort by buying war stamps. War stamps were available for purchase at the post office for 10 cents each, to be pasted into a booklet. It took $18.75 in stamps to fill a booklet, which was exchanged for a bond that would have a value of $25 when it matured in ten years. In essence, we would be loaning the U.S. government money to win the war. My dad offered us a deal. If we filled half a book ($9.40), he would pay the other half, and we could turn it in to get the $25 bond.

·   ·   ·

DAD BELIEVED that setting a goal and saving was important and also that the war effort was worthy of our participation. So I faced a dilemma every week. Should I put 10 cents of my allowance into the bank for the bike, or should I be patriotic and buy a war stamp. Should I save towards the bike, or join the block-long line of children buying tickets to see "Ma and Pa Kettle" at the local theater?

I did some of each, but in the end, by the time the war was over in 1945, I had purchased three war bonds. When the last of the bonds matured, ten years after the purchase, it was 1955. I had started teaching by that time, so my need for the money and the value of the money was not even close to what it was when I sacrificed and bought stamps at 10 cents each. The bonds just sat there in a file cabinet in my parents' home for a few more years, gaining some additional interest, but not much, and inflation stole away the value that money had when I invested it. It makes me sad now to think about little Barbara sacrificially giving up weekly treats, earnestly believing she was helping the country. And maybe she was. It was important for all of us to be part of the war effort.

My Dad's name was on the bonds as the secondary owner. When he died at age 67, it was 1971, and I had been married and teaching for quite a few years. When I came home for his funeral, I redeemed the bonds and gave the money to my mother. We didn't know how her finances would work out now that her breadwinner was gone. She gratefully accepted the money and tucked it away, knowing she would need it at some time in the future. There wasn't anything I could have spent the money on that would have been worth the sacrifice I had made to save those nickels and dimes. Giving it away was an expression of grief, grief that my dad was gone, and grief that the money no longer had the value we had put on it. I just wanted to be done with it.

Some months after we started saving money for the bike, my cash register bank recorded the total at $9.45. Patty and I had the 55 cents we needed, so we set the bank on the dining room table and hollered out a general invitation:

"Anybody who wants to see our bank door open, come and watch!"

My parents and Betty joined us around the table as Patty and I took turns feeding the remaining 55 cents into the bank. When the bank registered $10, the door of the bank did come unhinged as promised. We shook the money out of the bank, coins rolling all over the table and some onto the floor. Everyone helped by picking up coins, sorting the nickels, dimes and quarters into stacks. Betty helped with the final count of the coins. She added and re-added and the total always came up 45 cents short of $10. She had easily come up with her $5, and Mother could magically manipulate that grocery money whenever necessary, so her $5 was not a problem. It was a huge disappointment, for we didn't know how long it would take us to acquire the 45 cents we needed.

But Dad surprised us the next evening when he walked the blue and white bike home from the Coast to Coast Hardware down the Main Street sidewalk, past Tubby's Grocery and the gas station, crossing the side street, down one more block past Bastyrs' Hatchery, drawing knowing smiles from the people he met. He turned the corner to the left and guided that bike to our house at the end of the block. Whoops and hollers greeted him as we spotted him through the window, pausing underneath the large oak tree, the sun dappling through the leaves, moving shadows and sunlight on his grinning face and on the blue and white bike.

It was suppertime, but we ignored the aroma of our favorite goulash wafting from the kitchen as we took turns riding that bike on the street, from the tree outside our back

I am on the bicycle we bought together. Solveig Stortroen is with me.

door to the stop sign at the end of the block and back again. We could smell Dad's greasy overalls, a pleasant familiar odor, as he steadied the bike, inexperienced and wobbly as we were, helping us to get started. A line formed with neighbor kids also getting turns on the shiny new bike, riding one block and back again, until fireflies flashed reminders that it was getting dark and time to go in.

I have this image in my mind of even my mother being outside with us, standing there in her blue and white checkered housedress and rolled down nylon stockings—my mother who was a fixture in the house with her cooking and cleaning —and that this was a family project. It was such a happy time.

The memory is about more than just owning a new bike. It was the unity of our parents. Sometimes there was obvious tension between them, and it was unsettling. They did not ever verbally fight. They fought silently. These times were like silent waves that came in and went out without comment or explanation. But the day of the arrival of the bike was a day of celebration and unity, and we were proud of ourselves because each of us had a part in accomplishing a goal that had seemed out of reach. I felt our parents were also proud of us, something they were so hesitant to convey for fear we would get "the big head," meaning we would think too highly of ourselves.

Mother said she was going to learn to ride the bike after dark so the neighbors wouldn't see her. She was always concerned about "what would the neighbors think?" But she never got around to riding the bike. Dad took one turn on the bike at our urging, just to prove he could do it. He never rode it again, but it was heart-warming for us to see that he really cared about our having fun. Betty developed other interests and didn't ride much. Patty was a bit small for the bike right away but eventually she got a lot of pleasure out of it. But I *really* loved that bike. I used it until I graduated from high school, riding with friends all over town and even out in the country. I would never have guessed that $22.95 worth of metal and rubber and blue and white paint could provide so much pleasure, be a reminder of memories of good times with friends, and linger as a symbol of achieving a goal together as a unified family.

16

PIANO LESSONS AND PORCUPINE MEATBALLS

WHERE DO OUR DESIRES AND interests originate from? DNA? Family members? The books we read? Our friends? All of those influence us, but I am sure my desire to learn to play the piano originated from my friend Patsy Mattix. She had a piano in her house. She took lessons and practiced regularly. I wanted to do that, too.

My sixth grade picture

My sixth grade teacher Miriam Bakkum played the piano that stood at the front of our classroom when we did group singing. She was a kind person who showed interest in the lives of her students. She offered to teach me some basics about playing the piano after school if I would stay around after the other students had left. I thrived on the interest she showed in me and appreciated the piano lessons. But I would need a place to practice.

Enter Patsy's mom, Mrs. Mattix. They had built their new house about a block and a half away from the Slukey house, on the Main Street of Mahnomen. Mrs. Mattix offered to allow me to practice my lessons on their piano in their living room. A very generous offer, indeed. It is challenging enough to listen to one's own child practice scales and hit sour notes and linger too long over a note during practice time, but to endure it for a neighbor's child shows unexpected grace and generosity.

Enter Mrs. Margot Wells, a former Sunday School teacher and neighbor. About two months later, when Mrs. Wells was preparing to move out of her house, she offered to sell us her upright piano with the yellowed ivory keys at a very nominal price. Somehow my thrifty mother produced the $20 for the piano, and it became OURS! It looked amazing in the living room against the south wall of the Slukey house, far more elegant than its modest price implied! Included was a piano bench with storage for music books, which we did not have yet, but would acquire.

Something like a musical Mary Poppins, a piano teacher named Miss Lockwood seemed to appear from nowhere to give lessons. I don't where she lived. A petite woman, she walked on the gravel street to our house. She was probably in her fifties, quiet spoken, with an accent unlike ours. She was smartly dressed in a long wool coat and a cloche hat and arrived promptly at 5 p.m. every Tuesday. Mother made the comment under her breath that Miss Lockwood was a "funny duck."

After the piano lesson, she stayed for supper as her payment for the lesson. We always had the same menu: porcupine meatballs in tomato sauce along with mashed potatoes, a vegetable and glorified rice for dessert. Those meals were awkward as far as conversation was concerned. My dad thought meals were for eating, not talking, and didn't sense any obligation to make polite small talk, and the rest of us followed his example because we didn't know how to do anything else. The food was tasty and worth concentrating on, and the purpose was accomplished: a meal in exchange for a piano lesson. Miss Lockwood said I had music in my fingers, and that made me feel happy and made Mother feel it was all worthwhile.

Betty, two years older than me, also wanted piano lessons. "How come she gets lessons and I don't?" she asked angrily. Certainly a fair question. The older child should be the trailblazer and have privileges. The situation had just evolved for me, with friends coming forward to help me. And so it was a hurt for Betty and a guilty feeling for me.

So on lesson day, Betty did the next best thing to having piano lessons. She pulled her chair up behind the piano bench, stretched to sit tall to see everything Miss Lockwood was talking about, and intently watched the lesson from behind. And she diligently practiced daily what she had learned.

I was no piano virtuoso, but I continued with lessons that year from Miss Lockwood. A year or two later, after we moved into the house we bought, I had piano lessons from Sister Dorothea, one of the Catholic nuns who lived in the rectory two blocks south of us. I enjoyed weekly lessons and was nervous about annual piano recitals, which involved performing special compositions all dressed up in my best dress (with butterflies in my stomach). I progressed to the John Williams Grade Four Book by the time I graduated from high school. The greatest advantage of taking lessons for me was learning how to read music and being introduced to various kinds of music, including classics. And I enjoyed it.

Betty did have piano lessons while she was in high school, and she also had lessons as an adult after her children were grown, even taking part in piano recitals along with the younger students. Patty had piano lessons when she was in fifth grade but didn't really have much interest in it.

The piano lived on in Mother's house until a year before she moved out of her house, when she sold it to someone with young children. The piano was enjoyed by my siblings and me, our children, and even our grandchildren. For years it sat grandly in the sun room, behind the French doors off the living room, across from the couch filled with Raggedly Ann and Andy dolls made by Eleanor, and played mostly when the children came to visit.

As for the Porcupine Meatballs, I always had fond memories of that delicious dish. When I married, I prepared the dish for my husband. To my dismay, Harvey, who liked most every kind of food, didn't like it. He said he didn't like rice sticking out of his meatballs. I thought he must be mistaken because it was so good, so I tried the recipe a second time. He didn't like it. So it fell into the Discard Recipe category. I included the recipe here so you can decide for yourself. It lives on in my memory: Porcupine Meatballs baked in Mother's blue enamel roaster in the oven of the cookstove which was fueled by wood put in one stick at a time. Yum.

Porcupine Meatballs
    Prep time: 20 minutes Cook time: 1 hour
    5 servings
    ½ cup uncooked long grain rice
    ½ cup water
    1/3 cup chopped onion
    1 tsp salt
    ½ tsp celery salt
    1/8 tsp pepper
    1/8 tsp garlic powder
    1 pound ground beef
    2 T. canola oil
    1 can (15 oz) tomato sauce
    1 cup water
    2 T. brown sugar
    2 tsp Worcestershire sauce

Combine first 7 ingredients. Add the ground beef. Shape into meatballs. Brown in the 2 T. canola oil. Combine the tomato sauce, cup of water, brown sugar and Worcestershire sauce and pour over the meatballs. Reduce heat, cover and simmer 1 hour.

❄ 17 ❄

A SURPRISE

IT WAS EARLY SPRING IN 1943. MY MOTHER WAS STANDING IN front of the small mirror that hung over the wash basin in the kitchen, reaching up with both hands rolling her hair back, fastening the roll with bobby pins. The reach made her protruding tummy stand out. It was the first time I had noticed the bump. No one had told me she was pregnant. I patted her tummy and said, "You're getting so fat."

She answered, "I'm going to have a baby."

"You are!?" I said, incredulously, barely able to take in the good news.

As a teenager and much more knowledgeable about the facts of life, Betty was embarrassed her mother was pregnant. She expressed her displeasure in a scolding manner. "How could they think of having another child when there wasn't enough money to go around for the rest of us?" She must have had a better source of information about the birds and bees than I did. At the age of 12 I still wasn't sure how babies were made and was too shy to ask.

As the due date approached, the plan was that Betty, age 14, was going to stay home and cook meals for Dad. Patty and I, ages 8 ½ and 12, were to stay with Grandma and Grandpa Wang on the farm in rural Ulen during the birth process and the week-long stay in the hospital. So my dad drove us to the farm in our car in early July. Too early, it seems. But we didn't stay long. We got homesick, begged to go home, and Dad came to get us before Mother even experienced birth pains. I didn't remember how we managed to communicate our misery and our plea to come home, but Patty remembers writing a letter to Mother, begging them to come and get us. The letter probably was not mailed immediately since it had to be taken to the post office in Ulen, about five miles away. Anyway, we were happy to be back home in Mahnomen before the action started.

The baby was delivered on July 25 at the Mahnomen Community Hospital, alive and well, and it was a BOY! David Lewis Braseth was named after his proud father. There was much cause for rejoicing. I sensed my dad had been worried. What if Mother, at age 36, had not survived childbirth? How would he handle life without her as the manager of our household? But she did survive and we celebrated!

Never able to express his feelings very well, he made an attempt to tell us we were fortunate our mother came through the delivery safely and was going to be all right (which we had taken for granted anyway), and that we should appreciate her and try to be helpful. And so, we did.

The Mahnomen County Fair was on that last week in July, the annual event we had looked forward to for months. We had saved our allowance money for this event, planning to spend it on rides and maybe treats. Dad was feeling so happy about having a son and a healthy wife, that he took us to the fair and paid for both the rides and the treats! It was unforgettable.

In those days the hospital stay for mother and child was at least a week, maybe even ten days. We were allowed to stay at home by ourselves during the day. Dad always walked home on his lunch hour for a noon meal, so he kept in touch with us. I have no memory of the meals during that time, and Betty, who was assigned to be in charge, is no longer available to answer questions (Betty died February 19, 2019, at the age of 89). I do remember there was a hail storm with baseball size hail. We thought it was hilarious and ran outside in it, not realizing how dangerous being hit could be.

A couple of days after the birth, I walked about eight blocks to the Mahnomen Hospital to visit Mother and baby and fainted from the hospital odors. I stood at the end of Mother's bed, facing her with my back against the wall. I started to sway a bit, and before I knew what was happening, I fell in a heap on the floor. A flurry of activity, someone turned me over, sat me up, put my head between my knees, and I came to. Of course, Mother was alarmed. So was I! This was the second time I had fainted from hospital odors. Soon I regained my senses and was able to walk home.

EVERYONE WANTED to help with the baby at first—take little David for a ride in the buggy, feed him his bottles, etc. I told myself they will get tired of it and then I could take care of him as much as I wanted. My patience paid off and I had plenty of time with the baby.

We tried to be helpful. I can't remember cooking or learning to make bread. I do remember washing and wiping dishes and arguing which job was easier, and hanging up clothes on wash day. And now there was an additional load of laundry with cloth diapers and baby clothes in the wash also.

David grew up in a different era that the three of us. He never experienced sharing a house with strangers, outdoor toilets (even though there was one on our property), carrying in water, hand-me-down clothes (because he was a boy and we didn't have any hand-me-downs for boys), having siblings close to his own age to play with, buying triple ice cream cones for a nickel, sharing a bike with siblings. He could, however, attend the movies for free because Dad ran the movie projector at the local theater in David's growing up years.

He also didn't experience having Mother home every day, all day like we did. She was offered a position as cook's assistant in the hot lunch program at the school where her friends were in charge, so she worked from early morning until 2 p.m. weekdays. The extra income was nice but it was hard work and involved lifting heavy containers of food. There were plusses and minuses in being the tail-end child. David will have to tell you his own story. I just remember the joy he brought to our household that day in July, 1943.

David

18

A TALE OF TWO BLIZZARDS

THERE WERE TWO BLIZZARDS THE YEAR I WAS A FOURTH-grader. It was as if Mother Nature put double exclamation marks on both ends of the winter of 1940-1941: the Armistice Day Blizzard of 1940 and the Ides of March Blizzard of 1941. These events were not only remembered by those who lived through them. They were also given names and recorded in history.

BLIZZARD /ˈblɪzəd/ *noun.*
   a) a storm with dry, driving snow, strong winds, and intense cold. b) A heavy and prolonged snowstorm covering a wide area.[1]

These definitions seem like gross understatements to those who lived through either of the two events, both of which have been described with having up to 80-mile-an-hour winds with noises as loud as a train, paralyzing cold temperatures, and driving, blinding snow.

THE ARMISTICE DAY BLIZZARD OF 1940

The fall weather had been unseasonably warm in northern Minnesota in 1940, and temperatures were a balmy 50 degrees at 7:30 in the morning on November 11. Who would ever guess that extreme winter weather would be measured for generations by the Armistice Day Blizzard of 1940?

Hundreds of duck hunters enticed by the holiday and dressed for warm weather were thrilled by the masses of ducks flying low, migrating south. Many later reported that they had never seen so many birds. It was as if they knew something of which the hunters were unaware.[2]

The winds began to pick up, and then suddenly, it began to rain, and then temperatures dropped rapidly, turning the rain to sleet and then to blinding snow. Out on the lakes and in marshlands, hunters lost their chance to find their way safely to shore. Some drowned as 70-80 mph winds swept up waves, overturning boats. Others froze to death when the temperature dropped fifty degrees into single digits. Many that did manage to survive lost hands or feet from frostbite. It was known as "The Day the Duck Hunters Died." [3]

The storm cut a 1000-mile-wide path through the middle of the country from Kansas to Michigan. Motorists stuck in snowdrifts on remote stretches of road were buried alive in their cars, their frozen bodies found days later. Farmers checking their livestock became disoriented in the blinding snow and froze to death, some not far from their houses or barns. Before it was over, more than 150 people and thousands of livestock were dead.[4]

Armistice Day Blizzard Minnesota 1940. Courtesy Vintage News Daily

OUR FAMILY WAS cozy at home, perhaps listening to a radio program such as "Fibber Mcgee and Molly" or "The Lone Ranger," and except for the howling wind, we were mostly unaware of what Mother Nature was doing. Looking back, I feel fortunate that my dad, an avid hunter, was not out hunting. Very likely, he had to work on Armistice Day because he worked six days a week and rarely had time off.

The next day was Tuesday, and I naively expected to go to school. I don't remember how we heard if school was canceled in those days, but I know that we didn't hunker down around the radio, hoping to hear the name of our school in the list of cancellations. Mother simply said there could not be any school in such weather, but I was determined not to take any chances of spoiling my perfect attendance record, so I begged her to let me go.

"Puleeze."

Finally, she gave in and said:

"Oh, all right then. Put on your cap and mittens, snow-pants and coat and boots. And tie a scarf over your face."

I was already dressed in my cotton dress, long underwear, and long stockings held up by my garter belt—standard dress for winter.

All bundled up, I pushed hard to open the back door against the snowdrift on the porch. When I had an opening wide enough to squeeze through, I tried to find the steps through the deep snow. I struggled through the yard, leaning from side to side as I pulled my overshoe-clad feet out of the snow. Making my way to the end of the block, I looked up and down Main Street. There was no traffic. Silence. Huge drifts looked like modernistic sculptures. Even though it was only one more block to the school, I turned back and went home. There was not a human being in sight. Mother was right. There couldn't be school. I had not spoiled my perfect attendance record.

THE IDES OF MARCH BLIZZARD OF 1941

Mother Nature was not done playing tricks. As we approached the middle of March each year, we were beginning to "think spring." March 15 dawned a beautiful, warm day. Many had taken advantage of the sunshine to be out and about. Little did anyone know that the worst blizzard of the century was only hours away.

"The 'Ides of March blizzard' that struck from March 15-17, 1941, ranks as one of the worst in the Red River Valley's recorded history and one of the most disastrous ever nationwide. Over three days, the storm claimed the lives of 72 people, including 38 in North Dakota, 28 in Minnesota, and five in Canada," wrote Tracy Briggs in the March 13, 2019 issue of the Fargo Forum, recalling significant historical events. "The blizzard slammed into the valley virtually out of nowhere with the force of a tornado or a hurricane and turned what had been a bright, sunny, warm spring-like day into a raging nightmare."[5]

Like the November blizzard, there had been no warning, so people were not dressed warmly. Many were trapped in cars. Deaths resulted from people leaving stalled vehicles and trying to walk to safety

In rural Mahnomen, on March 15, a beautiful, sunny day, Pete and Clara Bjerken and their three children, Violet,

Arnold, and Palmer had been supper guests at the home of the Borgens, neighbors who lived about a mile from their farm. Violet, the fifth grader, was invited to stay overnight, so after supper the rest of the family expressed their thanks, said their goodbyes, and got into their Model A and drove away. About a quarter of a mile down the road they were suddenly met by a wall of impenetrable blizzard conditions.

Unable to drive further or turn around, they attempted to walk back to the Borgen home. Holding hands, struggling against the wind and biting snow, they became totally disoriented, turning into a field instead of the farm yard. After repeatedly stumbling, Mrs. Bjerken and seven-year-old Palmer collapsed, unable to continue. Twelve-year-old Arnold kept urging his father to get up and keep going. They eventually found refuge at the Alfred Larsen farm, about a mile and a half from the Borgen home, frostbitten and exhausted, but alive.

When the storm subsided, rescue teams, including my dad, were formed to go out looking for survivors. The mother and youngest son were found huddled together, frozen to death. In describing what the rescuers experienced, my dad gestured that the snow drifts were higher than their heads.

When we went back to school later in the week, we discussed the sobering news about the tragedy of the Bjerken family. Jean Bjerken, who was a member of our fourth-grade class, lost her Aunt Clara and cousin Palmer, who was a second grader. The whole second grade class attended his funeral. The entire Mahnomen community was shocked and saddened by this tragedy.

I KEEP THINKING that if they had left just ten minutes earlier, they might have made it home. If they had left just ten minutes later, the blizzard would have been upon them, and they would never have ventured out. What a difference ten minutes can make.

In the instances of both blizzards, you might wonder: Why didn't people listen to the weather forecasts? There wasn't much weather forecasting until years later. Practical use of numerical weather predictions began in 1955, spurred on by the development of the programmable electronic computer.[6] Unlike today, we were not bombarded by weather forecasts and reports. The weather just happened, and in these two instances, everyone was caught by surprise.

THAT WAS the winter we walked on the surface of the snow without breaking through, the hard crust glistening like a million diamonds in the sun. We had hours of fun digging tunnels underneath the hard surface, a network of passageways, a community underneath the snow. The trick Mother Nature had played on so many lives turned out to be a gift to us as it provided hours and hours of creativity and fresh-air fun and exercise for us. As in so many things in life, it all depends upon one's point of view.

1. www.dictionary.com
2. Washburn, L. (2008). The icy winds of death: The Armistice Day blizzard November 11, 1940. *Iowa Outdoors.* 67(5), 34-41.
3. Knarr, A.J. (1941, June). The Midwest storm of November 11, 1940. *Monthly Weather Review.* 69 (6). 169-178.
4. US Department of Commerce, NOAA. "Armistice Day Blizzard of 1940 Remembered." Accessed August 10, 2019. https://www.weather.gov/dvn/armistice_day_blizzard.
5. Tracy Briggs, The Fargo Forum, "Wayback Wednesday: Ides of March Blizzard," March 13, 2019.
6. Robbins, Chris. "A Brief History of Weather Forecasting." iWeatherNet, January 18, 2015. www.iweathernet.com/educational/history-weather-forecasting.

V

THE HOUSE WE BOUGHT

19

THE HOUSE WE BOUGHT

I KNOW NOW THAT BY 1943, THE GREAT DEPRESSION HAD come to an end due to World War II stimulating the economy, but I'm not sure we personally felt the effect. History reports that 18 million women were now employed in manufacturing in the big cities, but in the small town of Mahnomen my mother was still very busy taking care of her family at home, especially since she had a new baby.

We were already accustomed to sugar and tire rationing but now America saw its first rationing of canned goods, meat, cheese, butter and cooking oil. My mother's frugal cooking style wasn't so much affected by these limitations. Except for sugar. I really did not like Honey Jumble cookies taking the place of Mother's fabulous sour cream cookies made with sugar. Of course, she had to keep track of turning in stamps when she bought these items, but our fair share as determined by the Ration Board seemed to be almost enough for us.

The war in Europe turned the Allies' way, which was good news. My mother had two brothers serving in the US Navy, and a brother-in-law in the Seabees. All of that seemed far away.

Franklin Roosevelt was serving his third term as president of the United States, Winston Churchill was prime minister of the United Kingdom, Adolf Hitler was chancellor of Germany, and Stalin was general secretary of the Central Committee in Russia. I was only aware of who our president was because he spoke to the country regularly by his radio talks.

The once copper penny was now struck in steel because of a shortage of copper. Gasoline cost 15 cents a gallon, a new car $900, a new house $3600, and a bottle of Coca Cola cost 5 cents.

We were renting the Slukey house when Mother heard that the Blaskey house was for sale. That was the house to which I delivered the rent check every month when we first arrived in Mahnomen and lived in the Half House. It was the house Mother had dreamed of owning, but we never knew she was dissatisfied with the houses we rented.

"I want that house," she said to Dad. Rarely did she speak so directly.

"We can't afford it. We don't have the down payment. Just the down payment is $500," Dad said. Apparently, he was aware of her interest in that house, because he already knew the advertised price.

"Oh yes, we do," she said slyly. "I have been saving for this. I have it."

Saving nickels and dimes from the household money had paid off. Living in lower-rent houses expedited the savings process. Buying day-old bread saved one cent a loaf. Making meals out of duck and pheasant and venison and fish, often cleaning it herself, saved on the grocery bill. Sewing dresses from flour sacks for her girls saved even more money. Mother made a game out of saving—she was the queen of thrift. She had patience all those years and was ready when her dream house went on the market.

There had forever been a hesitation to make a down payment on a house, for fear of losing one's job and not being able to make the payments, and then losing even the down payment. It seemed risky. But they went ahead, and became proud owners of the Blaskey house, but ever after referred to as The House We Bought.

Tall oak trees stood like sentinels, spaced twenty feet apart across the front of the double lot that was our yard. A hedge on the north side provided privacy from the school property. A one-stall garage and a shed and an outdoor toilet bordered the west side, along with lilac bushes and a crabapple tree edging the garden. A fence separated our garden from the neighbor's garden on the south. These were the back yards we trespassed as little kids, avoiding the bullies from across the street as we went to school a few years earlier.

The House We Bought

We were already familiar with the wide-open porch from having delivered the rent check several years earlier. Now the house was ours and it was quite wonderful. On our first visit after the purchase, we excitedly explored the living room, the sunroom behind the French doors, the alcove room off the big dining room, the kitchen with its closet, the basement with the big furnace, the three bedrooms upstairs, the bathroom with the claw-footed bathtub. We ran helter-skelter all over the house, shouting to each other

"Look at this!"

"Look at that!"

"Who gets this bedroom?"

"Where will we put our stove?"

"Look, a sink on the wall—no more pumping water!"

"We have a furnace grate again!"

"Look at the back yard—there is a garden!"

It was here in this house that we once again became Front Door People. As we would exit the front door unto the gray wooden porch, we would be headed in the direction for school or church—if we turned left at the end of our sidewalk. If we wanted to head up town, we would walk straight ahead one block and then turn left onto Main Street. We came to love the new location and the ease in describing it. We were "the first house south of the school."

The back door was used most often for doing gardening chores, hanging up clothes on the clotheslines, or for a shortcut into the side entrance of the school. But mostly we were now Front Door People who had returned to their first neighborhood in Mahnomen.

The living room was sparsely furnished at first, but soon we acquired a rose-colored davenport, and a rug from Sears Roebuck that didn't quite match the furniture but was too big to send back. Our black rocker, a wooden painted captain's chair and the piano filled out the room. Mother had a knack for making a house into a homey place and was good at arranging pictures on the walls. Her treadle Singer sewing machine in the wooden cabinet found its niche in the alcove off the dining room. Later Dad acquired a grey metal desk to sit beside it and house his business papers.

When we bought the house, the dining room was fully furnished—if we had the $25 the sellers were asking. Mother had saved enough for that as well. The mahogany veneer dining room set included an extra wide table with leaves for extensions, a tall glass-doored china cabinet on legs, a wide buffet with drawers and doors for dishes and table cloths, and six wiggly, squeaky worn upholstered chairs. All of this looked so grand to me as it sat under the fancy light fixture in the dining room.

Now, 75 years later, I am remembering that dining room set. David and his childhood friend Robert Walswick recalled riding along with Mother and Dad to Fargo more than once, so Mother could shop for a new dining room set, which she never did buy. At age 90, Mother reluctantly left her beloved house to move into an apartment. That meant selling the furniture she could not take along, including the dining room set. In the intervening years, that which had been deemed old was now "antique." It had become valuable.

Two of Mother's granddaughters, Julie Johnson and Karen Polack, had warm memories of that furniture and wanted to acquire it and were willing to pay generously. But facing the challenge of shipping it to Texas or to New York, both of them decided against it. Karen did purchase the china cabinet and had it delivered to her in New York when Mother moved out of the apartment into the nursing home. She also saved the leaded glass window that looked onto the front porch from destruction. At her request, Betty had it removed and crated and shipped to her in New York. The buffet went to one buyer and the table and chairs to another, bringing in many times the amount originally spent on the whole set. This was another example of the transition from depression years to inflation years, and a change in the value of a dollar.

The house did not fare such a lovely ending. The school board had purchased the property from Mother when she was in her eighties, with the stipulation she could live there as long as she wanted, rent-free. They took care of mowing and snow removal, but they did not continue to invest in repairs because they were going to demolish it and landscape those two lots. The school superintendent was very sensitive to mother's feelings and they never urged her to move out. Even after she moved to the nursing home after living in the apartment for six years, they hesitated to demolish it while she was still alive, but she lived to 102 years old. She outlived their patience. When she was 98 years old, it was bulldozed down and covered over with sod. She saw it. She never said a word.

Now if you drive by the Mahnomen Public Schools, you will see sidewalks and grass and shrubbery gracing the front of the addition to the school, as if it had been there from the day the school was built. Few people know that buried beneath those walkways and lawn are broken beams and woodwork, shingles and plaster, shattered glass, 50's pink countertop, black and white linoleum (yes, we did remodel), gold carpet, and an old furnace. But not my childhood memories of The House We Bought. They are not buried there. They are safely held close in my heart.

20

MY FIRST REAL JOB

"WOULD YOU BE INTERESTED IN WORKING IN THE OFFICE OF The Mahnomen Pioneer this summer, Barbara?" The voice on the other end of the phone call belonged to Mrs. Clara Carver, owner, publisher, and editor of the local weekly newspaper. She was a distinguished member of the local community, sharp looking with her rimless glasses, fashionable clothes, and short greying haircut shaped at the nape of her neck. She lived with her two daughters in the apartment above the newspaper office at the north end of Main Street in Mahnomen. I was invited to come to her office to discuss the position.

Wow! Yes, I was interested! It was the summer after my junior year in high school. The pay was $15 per week, and I worked a regular five days a week schedule. My job was to answer the phone when Mrs. Carver was not there, taking ads and social news as I listened to the callers, and writing these items up for her approval. When we were short of social items from our correspondents, I was to call for news, such as "so and so visited so and so" or "Mr. and Mrs. Nameless have returned from a trip to Arizona ..." I also proofread the galleys on printing days, marking errors with standard proof-reading marks.

Linotype operater, Peter J. Adamson in the Swedish Tribune newspaper office, Seattle, Washington, February 1904. Courtesy of University of Washington Libraries, Special Collections

Every line of every column of print that appeared in the paper each week had to be entered on the keyboard of the linotype ("line of type") machine. Hot liquid metal was then poured into a mold created by the type that was set. Each line of type (a column width) became a metal bar about 1/8 of an inch by two inches by two inches called a "slug." If the proof-reader found an error on the galley proof, the "slug" that contained the mistake had to be pulled out, and a new one created on the linotype machine and slipped into its place.

A linotype slug. Courtesy of Gerhard Doerries..
ttps://commons.wikimedia.org

A tall, lanky young man named Don was the linotype operator for the Mahnomen Pioneer. He sat for hours in front of that noisy metal, clanking, banging machine each week, turning words into metal bars of type that would be used to print the weekly issue of the paper.

One of my favorite duties was proofreading. The printer prepared the galley proof copy by rolling ink over the shiny new type which had been laid out by pages on the tables in the press room. Putting newsprint paper down on it and pressing with a rubber roller, he allowed wide margins for the proofreader's marks, so I could indicate what corrections needed to be made. I loved doing this, but, understandably, Don did not enjoy making the corrections. No one likes to have their errors pointed out. Sometimes I found errors in the corrected slugs, and Don would have to remake a slug for the second time. Certainly, that was an example of when "haste made waste."

The commercial ads were set by hand and were the responsibility of another employee. The various sizes and fonts of type were kept in a compartmentalized wooden box called a type case. The typesetter moved quickly, picking each letter he needed out of the type case, setting it in place in the ad, upside down and reading from right to left.

My proofreading copy on paper read from left to right, but when I needed to look for the line that had errors in it (slug) to replace it with the corrected slug, I was reading upside down and from right to left. It became a natural skill after a while.

Press day was Wednesday afternoon, with The Mahnomen Pioneer available for distribution Thursday morning. It was an exciting time when we rushed to meet the deadlines, smelling the ink and hearing the printing presses rolling out the paper, assembling, and folding the sheets automatically, the culmination of the week's work. The newspapers were counted and bundled together to be distributed for sale to various business places around town. Some people came into the office to buy their copy for a nickel. One more edition was out to the readers!

The next morning, we dismantled the hand-assembled ads, leaving the framework of the ad to be filled with following week's specials. The next week's issue was underway. Newspaper work was constant. There was no significant break in the work cycle. As soon as we finished one paper, we would start the next.

The Mahnomen Pioneer office was at the end of the business district on Main Street. Upon entering the front door, to the left was the desk of Clara Carver, and to the right, behind the door, was my desk. Straight ahead through the open door was where all the typesetting and printing took place. I didn't have a phone at my desk, so when I was alone and answering the phone, or gathering news via phone calls, I often sat at Mrs. Carver's desk. She always entered the front office from the printing press door because her apartment was accessed from that side. One day I could hear her quick high-heeled footsteps as she approached the doorway into the front office and was aware that the clicking of her heels abruptly stopped when she saw me at her desk. I looked up from my work and quickly sensed I was in her space inappropriately. I was sensitive about using her desk after that. Personal territory is a subtle concept that we pick up by observation and experience. Sometimes we learn lessons without words ever being spoken.

Somewhere along the way, beginners are going to make bloopers. I got teased for one of the ads that I accepted over the phone. Someone wanted to sell 100 chickens, which were one year old. The ad I put in the Want Ad section read: "For sale: 100 year old chickens. Call 925-2222 if interested." I should have used hyphens for better clarity. I think my boss took some ribbing on the error. She reminded me that I was supposed to run those phone ads through her before sending them to the linotype operator. Lesson learned.

What a dream job for a high school student—lots of learning experiences, a great mentor and role model in Clara Carver, and a closeup look at the field of journalism as it played out in a small town. I liked the work and the field of work but I really didn't consider it as a career. I had my mind set on teaching, so my career in the newspaper industry was short-lived, but the experience left me with lessons learned, insights gained, and memories that have stayed with me for more than seventy years.

❧ 21 ❧

MY FIRST DRIVER'S LICENSE

To obtain a driver's license in 1947, when I was 16 years old, one had only to go to the courthouse and fill out an application. The local newspaper, The Mahnomen Pioneer, reported that a new law would take effect in 1948, and an applicant for a driver's license would have to pass a written test and a driving test. Several people said, "Why don't you get your driver's license now, while it is there just for the asking?"

When we lived in the House Up North, we walked by the Mahnomen County Courthouse every day when we went to school. The rust-colored brick building was centered majestically on a whole city block, with well-planned sidewalks and a hedge all around. It was just north of the Lutheran Church where we attended Sunday School and just south of the Mahnomen Hospital where my brother David was born. The outside of the building was familiar but I never had occasion to go inside until now.

I entered the impressive front door, stepping onto decorative tiled floors and faced a staircase right in front of me. I walked upstairs and found the Department of Motor Vehicles behind doors with frosted glass windows and identifying department names. Camilla Hardy came to the counter and greeted me by name. She was the organist of our church, a Sunday School teacher, the mother of one of my classmates, and the Clerk of Court.

"What can I do for you today, Barbara?"

"I came to get a driver's license," I responded hesitantly.

She left the room to get a form and came back, ready to write.

First question Mrs. Hardy asked was, "Can you drive a car?"

Panic set in. I could have said I was learning and that probably would have sufficed. But with all honesty, I answered, "No."

"Well, then, I cannot legally issue you a driver's license."

Embarrassed and red-faced, I left the courthouse, aware that I was now probably the butt of a joke and that I had a challenge ahead of me.

That evening I asked my Dad to teach me to drive. He said if I was really interested in driving, I would have been watching him as he drove and would know how to put the key in the ignition, how to shift the gears, etc. Clearly, I wasn't ready to learn to drive.

He was probably right. I didn't have a big desire to drive at that time and likely would not have had permission to drive his car anyway. I didn't really learn to drive until after I graduated from college, and I never owned a car until after I was married. It seems impossible now that the seven years I taught school before I was married, I was getting rides from friends or borrowing a car from my parents.

My granddaughter Katie learned to drive the golf cart when she was about five years old. When she got a permit to drive to and from school at age fourteen, her other grandparents gave her a car, and she had her driver's license by the time she was sixteen. Times sure have changed.

THE SCHOLARSHIP

"What do I want with talking to him?" My dad's voice was gruff, too loud. I was afraid he could be heard in the living room.

He had just entered the back door into the kitchen after walking home from a full day's work at his mechanic's job at Roy's Garage and Machine Shop. He was responding to my statement that there was a representative from Concordia College in the living room waiting to meet him. Still wearing his greasy, oily-smelling striped bib overalls and his hard-toed work boots, he was tired and not in the mood to greet someone he had no interest in. He stood a moment in the kitchen, so familiar with its worn furnishings, aware they should be replaced: the old cooking range, the second-hand refrigerator, the standalone cupboard, the chipped white metal-topped table, the sink hanging on the wall, all a reminder that we had been living frugally for years. Certainly we were not ready to undertake college bills.

Minutes earlier a gentleman from Concordia College, a professor in the business department, who was also serving as a recruiter, had arrived at our front door, introducing himself as Ivan Larson. He was tall, neatly dressed in a blue-grey suit, red tie, rimless glasses, wearing a pleasant smile, and was looking for Barbara Braseth, the salutatorian of the graduating class of 1949. He had come to offer me a $50 scholarship towards second semester tuition at Concordia College in Moorhead, Minnesota.

To me, it sounded like an opportunity to fulfill my dreams. I had secretly hoped I could attend Concordia College, so it was a lifeline to have someone from the college approach me. In 1949, the year I graduated from high school, we had no guidance director at Mahnomen High School, no one on the staff to help us with career goals and guidance as to how to achieve those goals. So I didn't even know how to begin the application process. Since childhood I had said I was going to be a teacher, but had no practical plans to achieve that dream.

My sister Betty, two years older than I, had attended Moorhead State Teachers College, taking a one-year course that qualified her to teach in a rural school. She was teaching now on a four-month assignment, renting a room and living in the home of a school board member during the week, with only a curtain separating her bedroom from the family living quarters. She had full responsibility for teaching all subjects, first through eighth grade, in that one-room school, including janitor chores, such as keeping the fire going in the furnace. She had no car, so my dad went to get her on weekends and then take her back to her teaching life on Sunday night.

Betty was outgoing, a creative, loving teacher, and enjoyed her work, but it was a very restricting life with little privacy for a twenty-year old. As the oldest in the family of four children, she was our trailblazer, but I wasn't interested in teaching in a country school. I was hoping to attend Concordia College, in large part because it was a Christian college and because it could open doors for my future.

I had been on a spiritual journey of sorts ever since attending Sunday school as a four-year old, going through Lutheran confirmation, memorizing the catechism and its meaning, participating in Luther League, and attending the International Luther League Conventions in Milwaukee and Saskatoon, Canada. I was looking forward to making friends with people of similar values and growing my faith while training my mind. I was also looking forward to making a fresh start because, although by outward appearances I had had a successful high school career, I was shy and had had very little dating experience. I had never even been on the Concordia campus, but somehow I had my heart set on attending Concordia College.

My dad reluctantly followed me through the dining room and into the living room towards the guest, feeling trapped into greeting someone who represented a college he was not pleased to have his daughter considering. Mr. Larson eagerly moved towards us, extending his hand towards my dad, inviting a handshake, as I introduced them.

"Pleased to meet you, Mr. Braseth."

Dirty and tired from a long day's work, my dad was grumpy and inhospitable. He looked at the visitor's well manicured hand and then down at the palms of his own dirty, greasy hands. He rubbed them against his dirty overalls, looked at them again, and dropping his hands to his sides, glancing downward, he muttered, "I'm too dirty to shake hands."

Mr. Larson graciously said, "I understand. Maybe I came at a bad time. I just wanted to tell you that your daughter is good college material, and we would like to offer her a scholarship and invite her to become a student at Concordia."

Shaking his head slowly from side to side, looking downward and avoiding eye contact, my dad replied, "It's too expensive for us." He turned and went back to the kitchen.

I was embarrassed at my dad's lack of social graces. But Ivan Larson assured me that the scholarship would be there for me to apply towards second semester tuition if I found a way to come to Concordia. He left me his business card and was soon on his way to the next town, searching out other candidates for his $50 scholarships, girls and boys who had the highest grade-point averages in their graduating classes.

My father's objection to my attending Concordia College was all about money. Too expensive. Admittedly, he was completely justified. He had worked hard six days a week the past twenty years, supporting his family as a mechanic and taking on repair jobs in the evening to earn extra money. For the past six years he had successfully made payments on our house. To even be buying a house seemed risky to people coming through the Great Depression. There was always a fear of losing one's job and then not being able to make the payments, which would result in forfeiture, loss of original investment. For seven years prior to that, he had moved his family in and out of rental homes, with rent payments ranging from $17 to $25 per month, homes that did not even have indoor plumbing. So to consider paying college expenses for a liberal arts education at an estimated cost of $300 for the semester for daughter number two was not in his plan.

If it were today, we would think the logical solution would be for me to take out a loan to pay for my education, but there were no college loan programs at that time. The earliest ones began in the late fifties and became more available in the sixties. We lived on a cash basis. No credit cards. If you didn't have the cash, you did without.

I did have two good summer jobs, at the local newspaper office and at the school superintendent's office, but at the going rate of $15 a week, it was impossible to accumulate savings that would make a significant dent in the cost of attending Concordia College. So after Ivan Larson's visit, I asked my dad a couple of times if I could attend Concordia just one year, and then I would take a civil service test and get an office job.

"Please. Just one year."

I did have marketable office skills which I had learned in

high school: typing, Gregg shorthand and transcription. I had successfully worked at a short-term job for a lawyer, taking dictation and transcribing notes at a trial in the courtroom. I had the skills to start work immediately in an office. But I wanted to go to Concordia.

"Please. Just one year."

At some point that summer, he said "yes." Grudgingly, of course.

Concordia College in Moorhead, Minnesota

In September 1949 Dad moved me and my belongings to Concordia in Moorhead, Minnesota, 75 miles from Mahnomen, into South Hall, a two-story dorm on campus. My first year at Concordia College was filled with learning experiences and challenges. I made some lasting friendships in the dorm and also in classes. We were introduced to dorm rules: lights out at 10:30 p.m., study hours enforced week nights from 7:30 to 10:30 p.m. requiring freshmen to be in the dorm, with one night out during the week. There were bed checks every night and curfews on weekends with doors locking at midnight. Violators were campused for two weeks. No dancing allowed. It was an adjustment, but it was harder for a lot of freshmen than it was for me. It fit my introverted life style and felt safe for me. I was happy to be at Concordia.

As I signed up for my courses, I had the idea I should round out my education. So instead of building on my strengths, I challenged myself by filling in weak areas. Bad idea. Freshmen were required to take either math or science. I had a good math background but had not taken much science in high school. So I enrolled in biology and struggled, especially with the labs scheduled right before supper. Formaldehyde fumes still remained in my nostrils as I ate the cafeteria food.

For the most part, I thought the cafeteria food was delicious, but learned not to say so because people wondered where I had come from. Not that my mother wasn't a good cook or that I had ever gone hungry. And even though the abundance and the choices were tempting to me, I made a big effort to choose wisely and make my semester's meal ticket last as long as possible.

MEANWHILE, another scholarship recipient—a redhead with an engaging smile from Tolley, North Dakota—showed up on campus in January. Harvey Johnson had the highest grade point average of all the boys in the Tolley High School Class of 1949. Actually, he was the *only* boy in that graduating class of seven students. He had finished helping with the fall harvest as a ranch hand on the McCarroll Ranch where he had worked summers for the past five years, and then completed a three-month job working on the railroad, replacing railroad ties. By Christmas, he was wondering what to do next. Remembering the Concordia scholarship and accepting the offer of the ranch family to lend him some money, he arranged for the local pastor to give him a ride to the train station, where he boarded a train to Moorhead. He enrolled at Concordia starting the second semester, simply because the opportunity had presented itself to him in the form of a scholarship.

Harvey's College Graduation picture

A year or so later Harvey invited my roommate and me to his apartment above the Hanson-Runsvold Funeral Home in Fargo where he had part-time employment, and he and a friend of his served Mary Ellen and me a home-cooked fish dinner. Harvey and I didn't have any other dates while at Concordia, but when we reconnected six years later, I discovered he didn't remember that first date. I found out why fifteen years later, when we were married, with family, and he was head of the biology department at Waldorf College.

He had arranged for other college biology instructors to come to Waldorf for a seminar, among them Phil Reiten, head of the biology department at Luther College and formerly one of his roommates at Concordia. His wife accompanied him, and when we were having lunch at our home, Ruth said, "Hey Harvey, remember that time you had me over for fish dinner at the funeral home?" Aha. I wasn't the only one to have such a date with Harvey. Apparently it was a standard low-budget date with a number of girls, so many he apparently couldn't keep track.

I ENROLLED in accounting without having taken accounting in high school. The professor moved steadily through the concept of debits and credits, and I fell behind in the class, a new experience for me. We had long columns of figures to add. The electronic calculator would not be invented for another 17 years, and I did not own an adding machine. If we planned ahead, we could get

My College graduation picture

into the business department when it was open during class hours and use their adding machines, but if we were working late at night finishing up homework, we were on our own. I became adept at adding but not adept enough. I talked to the instructor about dropping the course, but she urged me to keep going.

I finished my freshman year and talked my parents into letting me go back for the fall semester to brush up on my business skills and then take the civil service test. My dad agreed. So now I was in contact with Ivan Larson again, the recruiter who had come to our house. I took several business courses from him, and he became my advisor. He pulled me aside and pointed out how, if I became a business teacher instead of a secretary, my earning power would be much greater. His encouragement helped me to renew my desire to get my degree and become a teacher. And so, with my dad's permission, I continued on yet another semester.

I worked in Fargo the summer after my sophomore year. I shared an apartment with some friends and had a typing job at the Department of Supervised Study, which provided opportunities for high school students to take courses by correspondence. At the end of the summer I was offered a full-time position there, but figured out that by taking one college course by correspondence and 19 credit hours per semester, I could finish my college degree at Concordia in just three more semesters. I was more than half done! I asked for help *yet again* from my dad, to let me go ahead and finish. And once again, he agreed. The "Just One Year" had somehow turned into three and one-half years. It was seemingly impossible for him to express love and affection in words, but I see now the extent to which he showed it by his actions semester after semester. Years later he was heard to say, "It wasn't easy, but I'm glad we did it."

IN CONTRAST to my story of repeatedly asking for financial help from my parents, Harvey's story was one of grit and determination to do it himself. He had no other resources. He had so many practical skills which he learned from working on the McCarroll Ranch ever since he was twelve years old, he never seemed to have trouble finding a job. One winter day when he was down to a few dollars, and it had just snowed heavily, he bought a shovel and went door to door in the residential area near campus, seeking jobs shoveling sidewalks. He made enough money to meet his expenses for a few more weeks. By this time he had decided he wanted to become a coach and was determined not to let anything get in his way.

I graduated from Concordia in January 1953 with a BA degree, double major in Business Education and English, and started teaching high school business education that same month in Battle Lake, Minnesota. I finished out the year for a business teacher who had resigned because she was pregnant. At that time, pregnant women were not allowed to teach. How far women's rights have evolved! My salary was based on an annual salary of $3,000 per year, so I earned $1500 less taxes for that semester. I was rich!

❧ 23 ❧

PAYING IT FORWARD

AFTER COMPLETING A SECOND FULL SCHOOL YEAR OF teaching in Battle Lake, I was ready to start paying back what my parents had done for me. My dad had never mentioned re-payment, so instead of paying him back in cash, I offered to pay for remodeling the kitchen for them. Both parents benefitted from this. My mother got a new "fifties style" kitchen with black and white linoleum on the floor, pink countertops with a built-in double sink, black canisters decorated with pink roosters, and a new electric stove. Our big cooking range, after all those years of service, was now retired to a shed behind the house. In addition, my dad gained a special room for his new gun repair business, which was created by adding a wall during the remodel process. Everyone was happy with the changes, and I felt like I had made a positive contribution to the family after being on the receiving end so many years.

My mother in her new "fifties" kitchen in The House We Bought

This was the house that had been my mother's dream house, the house to which I delivered the rent check as a child for three years to the owners, the Blaskeys, when we were living in the half-house situation two doors south. This was the house for which she secretly saved enough money for the down payment and was prepared with her nest egg when the house went on the market.

I wondered how much the house cost back in 1942. My sister Pat remembered: $2700. I realized for the first time that what they spent on my college education (seven semesters times $300) was three-fourths of the cost of their house, an investment for which they had saved nickel by nickel. They had been buying day-old bread because it cost ten cents instead of eleven cents a loaf. And I was asking them to pay $300 a semester for my college education.

Why didn't I see it at the time? No one talked about finances but both parents were very frugal. All through my years at home, there always seemed to be enough for the essentials. When we bought this house, my mother purchased the dining room set left by the previous owners. It was a grand old set of furniture, filling the room with a mahogany veneer over-sized dining room table, a wide buffet with drawers and doors, a china cabinet perched on knobby legs and claw feet, with a large glass window revealing china cups and saucers, and six somewhat creaky, wooden chairs.

She outfitted the bay window with sheer Priscilla curtains ordered from the catalog, and added red geraniums in pots on plant stands. It looked beautiful to me. It is true the living room couch was shabby and a bit saggy with worn-out springs, and the thinning area rug didn't quite match the furniture, but the double French doors with the small glass panes leading into the sunroom off the living room added an air of sophistication, I thought. My mother created a cozy atmosphere. She was always home, and we could expect good aromas coming from the kitchen. My friends were always welcome. I felt rich. I didn't know we were poor.

So even though I felt regret at having taken advantage of their sacrifice, I can't imagine any other ending to the story for me. My Concordia experience seemed so right, and it led into a career area that was satisfying. Somehow my parents were also able to finance college degrees for my younger sister and brother in the years that followed. Earlier Betty had completed a two-year teaching degree at Moorhead State Teachers College, was married, and taught school for several years before choosing to stay home with her children. I guess it was all part of The Plan.

My dad enjoying the newspaper in the living room of The House We Bought

I could never fully repay my parents for their sacrifice and love. And so we pay it forward and give love and support to our own children in their varied career paths. And we provide college savings accounts for our grandchildren. In the end our parents were happy with the accomplishments of all their children. That is one of the joys of life—seeing one's children educated and well prepared to earn a living.

And I like to think that the $50 scholarship indirectly linked me with that scholarship recipient from Tolley, North Dakota, who six years after college graduation became a loving husband for me in a life journey that was fulfilling. Without that scholarship, perhaps neither of us would have found our way to Concordia College and would never have met.

History has a way of repeating itself. Our first-born daughter, Julie, met her future husband, Felix, through a Fulbright scholarship program that brought them together for a year of study in Vienna, Austria. Who knows what the future holds for the next generation? Or the next?

A BRIEF FAMILY HISTORY

When Abraham Lincoln signed the Homestead Act in 1862, he was sending out an invitation to the world to come to American shores. One hundred sixty acres was given to anyone who could pay a small filing fee and settle on the land for five years. When word reached Norway that land could be had for free, many made the hard decision to leave their homeland for new opportunities in America.

Among those immigrants responding to the invitation were my grandparents on my father's side, Bendick O. Braseth and Lise Haug, and my great-grandparents on my mother's side, Ellen and Elling Wang.

THE BRASETH FAMILY HISTORY

My dad's father, Bendick Braseth, was born in Aafjord, Trondheim, Norway on October 12, 1862. Bendick's mother had died when he was a child, and he came to America in 1881 with a group of young men. He eventually made his way to Ulen, Minnesota, to find work.

My dad's mother, Lise Haug, was born in Ringerykke, Norway, July 4, 1866. She came as a 10-year old girl along with three siblings, her widowed mother, Gunhild Haug, and her aunt and two uncles, arriving in America in 1876. The young family also settled in the area around Ulen, Minnesota, where they built a small house on homestead property with the help of neighbors.

Bendick and Lise were married on December 13, 1887. They purchased the homestead property from Lise's mother. Lewis, my father, was born December 21, 1903, the sixth of nine children. That same house was the house I came to know as Grandma Braseth's Farm, but my dad always called it The Home Place.

*THE BRASETH FAMILY Front row: Bendick, Amanda,
Gina, Lise holding Lewis Back row: George, Bertha, Oscar*

Our Grandpa and Grandma Braseth—Bendick and Lise Braseth

THE WANG FAMILY HISTORY

On my mother's side, it was my great-grandparents who immigrated from Norway. Elling Frederickson Wang was born February 25, 1844, at Inderoy, North Trondelag, Norway. Ellen Olsdatter Rost was born March 7, 1849, at Leksvik, North Trondelag, Norway. Elling Wang and Ellen Rost were married April 19, 1870, at Leksvik and left that spring for the "New World."

Elling and Ellen Wang's wedding picture

They first settled in Pennsylvania, then moved to Chicago, and eventually homesteaded in Hagen Township near Ulen, Minnesota. Their fifth child, Bernard E. Wang, my grandfather, was born March 12, 1879 in a dugout, their first home on this homestead property. Bernard attended school through fifth grade and then worked on his parents' farm where he leaned carpentry and farming skills.

THE FUGLIE FAMILY HISTORY

My other set of great grandparents, Ole and Jennie Fuglie, also immigrated from Norway. Ole A. Fugle came to the United States at age 5 in April 1870 with his parents, Amjor and Ole Arneson from Valdres, Norway. Ole homesteaded in Hagen township with his wife Jennie Meyer, whom he had married in Zumbrota in 1876. He went into the hardware business and later, when I knew him, he served as postmaster in Ulen, Minnesota. Ole and Jennie had six children, one of whom was my grandmother, Clara Mabel Fuglie, who was born September 7, 1888.

Our Grandma and Grandpa Fuglie as I remember them - Jennie and Ole Fuglie

Bernard and Clara were married on August 8, 1905. In 1910 they moved to his parents' homestead, which is the farm place we referred to as The Wang Farm when we visited as children. Eleanor, my mother, was born December 7, 1907, the second of nine children.

Bernard and Clara (Fuglie) Wang

Our Grandpa and Grandma Wang as I remember them —
Bernard and Clara Wang

LEWIS BRASETH AND ELEANOR WANG

The Braseths and the Wangs lived on homestead farms on opposite sides of the Wild Rice River in Clay County, Minnesota. A bridge connected those farms, and also two farm kids in their twenties, born to first and second-generation Norwegian immigrants.

Eleanor Wang, my mother, lived on one side of the river, and Lewis Braseth, my father, lived on the other. I like to wonder if Eleanor and Lewis ever met on that bridge. It is quite possible because, at some point, they fell in love and eventually married in November 1928.

Lewis Braseth

Lewis had many interests and was especially gifted in figuring out how things worked. His formal education went through eighth grade, but after they were married, he took a training course in auto mechanics at the Hansen Auto School in Fargo, North Dakota.

Eleanor Wang

Eleanor had attended country school through eighth grade and finished her high school education at Ulen High School, staying at Grandpa Fuglie's in Ulen to attend school. After high school graduation, Eleanor was enrolled in Moorhead State Teachers College for a one-year course that somewhat prepared her for teaching in a country school. She tried teaching that fall, dealing with an over-crowded school and unruly eighth-grade boys. She gave it up to get married to

Lewis. They were married in the church parsonage in Ulen that November.

Lewis and Eleanor (Wang) Braseth

After Betty was born on April 12, 1929, the young family moved to Twin Valley, Minnesota, a small town where most citizens were of Scandinavian descent. I was born there two years later, on April 18, 1931.

By that time, my dad had finished a training course in auto mechanics at Hansen Auto School in Fargo, North Dakota and had a job as a mechanic. A better job opportunity attracted him to the neighboring town of Mahnomen, and he was hired on as a mechanic We moved to Mahnomen when I was three and Betty was five.

Two years later, my sister Pat was born on November 24, 1934. Another 11 years would go by before David was born on July 25, 1943.

The story continued to unfold as each of us married and had children of our own, who in turn had families and exciting adventures of their own. I leave the telling of those stories for another time.

ACKNOWLEDGMENTS

I had thought often about recording memories of my childhood, but I didn't get started working on it until I was part of a college course on writing memoirs. In September 2017, Professor Tim Bascom, Chairman of the Creative Writing Program at Waldorf University, Forest City, IA, opened his class to members of the community. Auditing his course both semesters turned out to be an exciting adventure and great learning experience for this 85-year old retired business education teacher. Tim read all of our assignments carefully and thoughtfully and made valuable suggestions for improvement and revision. I am very grateful to Tim Bascom for his teaching and his help and encouragement.

During the two semesters my classmates were three other nontraditional students and seven traditional students: Joy, Cathleen, Bob, Dani, Diana, Isabelle, Myriah, Willie, Sam, and Jon. We read each other's work and made suggestions to each other. I learned from all of them. I remember what they wrote, what they shared of their lives, their giftedness, and the feedback they gave me. I am grateful to each of them. Joy Newcom did an extra favor by reading and proofreading the first copy of this book. A shout-out thank you to Joy!

Thank you also to family and friends who read chapters and gave me encouragement—my children: Julie Johnson, Jenny Johnson Conrad, Eric and Kristin Johnson. Thanks also to my sisters for providing information and feedback: Pat Bramel and Betty Polack. I also want to express gratitude to nephews Curt Polack and Stu Polack, and niece Beth Leintz, for reading my earliest essays and asking for more. And thanks to granddaughter Isabel Tweraser for help with book cover design.

A huge thank you to my editor and master of re-writing, my daughter Jenny Johnson Conrad, who never gave up on getting this through the rewriting and publishing process. She was knowledgeable and driven, an encouraging taskmaster who saw it through to the end. Thank you, Jenny!

I am grateful for keepers of history of those early years: the contributors to *Spanning the Century, The History of Ulen, Minnesota, 1886-1896*, published by the Ulen Union, c. 1985. It was a great resource for information about my great grand-parents and the early homesteaders. *The Fuglie Family History 1995* assembled with photos by Winton L. Fuglie was also extremely helpful. Thank you also to Jean Bjerken Hansen, a high school classmate from Mahnomen, who clarified details of the Ides of March blizzard as it pertained to her family members. Thank you to Katelyn of the Concordia College Library Archives in Moorhead, Minnesota, for refreshing my memory on what college actually cost for the 1949-1953 school years.

As I look back now, I see that times were hard when I was growing up in the 30s and 40s, and yet my childhood felt carefree. I am grateful for the parents I had and the life we lived.

Barbara Braseth Johnson

barbjohnson104@gmail.com

Made in the USA
Columbia, SC
26 November 2019